EMIGRATION
and
THE ADVENTURES OF A YOUNG ENGINEER IN CANADA

(1907-1914)

Volume 2
of
THE COLOURFUL LIFE OF AN ENGINEER
Memoirs of Harry Chickall Lott MC

As Peter Scott wrote, of himself, in his autobiography:
"I am, without question, the luckiest, and I believe, the happiest
man I know."

Grosvenor House
Publishing Limited

This book is published by
Grosvenor House Publishing Ltd
Link House
140 The Broadway, Tolworth, Surrey, KT6 7HT.
www.grosvenorhousepublishing.co.uk

A CIP record for this book
is available from the British Library

ISBN 978-1-83975-321-3

About the Author

Harry was a descendant of the Lott family who, for 200 years, had farmed at the Valley Farm and Willy Lott's Cottage in Flatford, made famous by Constable's paintings. In 1890 his father left farming and invested in a foundry business, Lott & Walne, in Dorchester where Harry attended Dorchester Grammar School and won a scholarship to study Engineering at the Central Technical College in London.

He first saw Canada on an Atlantic cable laying expedition in 1905 and emigrated there in 1907, where he worked as an inspector on the construction of bridges and hydro-electric schemes in five provinces, living in Montreal, Toronto and Winnipeg and in construction camps in the back-woods.

He returned to England in 1914 to join up for WWI and served in the trenches with the Royal Sussex Pioneer Regiment. He was promoted to the rank of Major after the battles of the Somme and Passchendaele where he was wounded. He was transferred to the Royal Engineers and, after the clearance of the battlefields in 1919, he was posted to the British Army of Occupation in Mesopotamia where he was appointed Lieutenant Colonel in charge of Mechanical & Electrical Services in Baghdad and Basra.

Harry returned to England on the Empress of Canada's first Round-the-World cruise in 1924 and joined Balfour Beatty Co. Ltd. in London for whom he worked as a consulting engineer until he retired aged 72 in 1955.

In the 1920's and 30's he carried out surveys for hydro-electric schemes for the East African Power and Lighting Company in Kenya, and undertook assignments in India and Nigeria as well as another round-the-world trip beginning with a journey to China on the Trans-Siberian Railway to submit a bid for the Shanghai Municipal Electricity Department.

His memoirs describe a remarkable life full of adventure and good luck. He did not marry until he was 59 and had a son Brian, who has edited these memoirs, adding some historical background and other items of interest from the diaries which Harry kept from 1900 until he died in 1975 aged 91.

Preface

These memoirs were originally written, or rather typed using an old-fashioned Smith-Corona typewriter, by my father, Harry Lott during his retirement from the late 1950's until a year before he died aged 91 in May 1975. He had kept daily diaries from 1900 until a week or so before he died, as well as numerous personal papers, photographs, menus, cuttings, reports, and letters. These provided source material for the several volumes of memoirs he wrote covering his first 50 years, up to the mid-1930's, when he considered that the 'colourful' years of his life had come to an end. By then he had become frustrated that his company, Balfour Beatty, no longer sent him on interesting overseas assignments but instead kept him office bound in London, using his extensive international experience and engineering judgement to evaluate and comment on the various new projects and business opportunities which came their way.

Having essentially completed his memoirs he asked a writer and journalist, Peter Ford, for his opinion on their suitability for publication. Peter thought that they were full of interest and suggested that they would benefit from the inclusion of more personal comments on the various individuals mentioned and that some links to current events of the day would add context. As a consequence my father added many inserts into the text and extra pages of anecdotes and detail wherever he could, with the result that, without the benefit of a word processor, the memoirs became even more like a scrap-book which no-one would ever read.

I inherited his memoirs, 75 years of his diaries and a filing cabinet full of his papers, photograph albums and other memorabilia. Whilst sorting through all these documents for archiving or disposal I decided to edit his memoirs, put them on a word processor and prepare them for publication in the hope that they may be of interest to future generations. During this process I added some extra material from my father's diaries and personal papers and I also inserted some historical background details in places, however, the majority of the content is exactly as he wrote it.

In preparing these memoirs for publication I decided to split them into five separate volumes, each dealing with a different chapter of my father's life. All five parts, if published together, would result in a book of a size which would put off most readers. If edited to remove many of the details, then each part would be of less interest to anyone reading it as a historical document. I can imagine my children, grand-children and possibly their descendants being interested in picking up a particular volume on, say, Canada, Mesopotamia or World War I and reading that, whilst not being prepared to tackle all five volumes at any one time.

The second reason is that, outside the family, each volume has potentially a quite different readership. Some readers or historical researchers may be interested in one or two of the volumes but not in all of them. The following summary of the contents of each volume provides an over view of the memoirs as a whole and enables readers to determine their interest or otherwise in the other volumes.

My father was an engineer, an officer and always a gentleman. He had a remarkable life and an interesting and varied international career in engineering during the first 30 years of the 20th Century. After 59 years of independence as a bachelor, he married my mother in 1942 and, in his last three decades, was a wise and wonderful father to me, despite being 60 years my senior. This work is my tribute to him. It has been a real pleasure re-living his experiences, researching stories of the people he met, the places he visited and the engineering history he describes. I hope that it will be of some interest and inspiration to my family, his descendants, and future generations of engineers.

J Brian Lott OBE
London, 2020

The Colourful Life of an Engineer
Volumes 1 to 5

Contents

The Colourful Life of an Engineer
Volume 2

Emigration
and
the Adventures of a Young Engineer
in Canada

(1907-1914)

Introduction

In the first volume of my memoirs I described my family roots in Flatford at the Valley Farm and Willy Lott's Cottage, made famous by John Constable in his painting of the Haywain, and my childhood memories of life and society in East Anglian farming villages in the late 19th century.

The agricultural depression of the 1880s and the growth of agricultural machinery businesses led my father to leave farming and try his hand at engineering in 1890. He invested in an iron foundry, Lott & Walne, in Dorchester where my schooldays were spent at the Dorchester Grammar School and my interest in nature developed on field trips in the area. I was musical and enjoyed playing the piano, becoming organist of our local church at the age of 15, a position I held until I obtained a scholarship to study Engineering at the Central Technical College in London.

After a very frugal three years in digs and at college in London, at a time when many new and exciting engineering developments were taking place, I was employed for a short time as a private tutor to Cyril Skinner who was working for a place to study engineering at Cambridge. However, my first real job was with a consulting engineering firm which sent me on the Atlantic cable laying expedition in 1905. During that trip, whilst our ship was being repaired in Halifax, Nova Scotia, I made a brief visit to Quebec City, Montreal, Toronto and Niagara Falls and fell in love with Canada. It was a young country with many opportunities for a young man and I decided to return.

Before leaving England I thought that I should obtain some practical experience as an electrical engineer and so I joined Marshalls of Gainsborough and spent 18 months in their workshops. It was hard work but stood me in good stead when I was looking for my first job in Canada. Having obtained my father's permission to emigrate, I left Liverpool on the SS Victorian in July 1907 and my experiences in Canada are the subject of this Volume 2.

I had just turned 24 when I arrived in Montreal with a ship-load of other immigrants, only a few pounds in my pocket and no job to go to. I obtained an introduction to Allis Chalmers Bullock and worked in their high-tension testing department for a few weeks on extremely low pay before moving to the Canadian Inspection Company where I was employed as an inspector of steelwork, mainly for bridges, in Nova Scotia, Quebec, Manitoba and Ontario.

As well as some of the engineering challenges I faced, the following pages of this volume describe the life of a young man in Montreal, Winnipeg and Toronto in those early years of the 20th century. After a 3-month holiday visiting family and friends in England in the summer of 1909, I returned to Winnipeg and joined the firm of Smith, Kerry and Chace who were consulting engineers for the new hydro-electric power plant at Pointe du Bois and the 77 mile transmission line being erected to supply its power to Winnipeg.

As an inspector on the erection of the transmission line I spent most of the next two years living in a tent in the back-woods north-east of Winnipeg in the construction camps along the line. These times, interspersed with short visits to civilisation in Winnipeg, were some of the most interesting of my career. As well as descriptions of life and work during winter and summer in the construction camps, there were adventures involving canoe trips on the Winnipeg river from Lac du Bonnet to Fort Alexander and moose hunting expeditions with an Indian guide which have left lasting memories.

During 1911, when my work on the transmission line had come to an end, I spent a few months supervising drilling work being carried out on the North Saskatchewan river to locate a suitable site for a new hydro-electric dam and power house to serve Prince Albert. The drill cores did not find rock competent enough for the foundations of a new dam and we recommended against the scheme. The Prince Albert city engineers decided to proceed with their project but the costs escalated and work on the La Colle Falls dam was eventually abandoned in 1916 when it was only half built and the city ran out of money.

After another trip home in spring 1912 I returned to Canada with Cyril Skinner, whose mother had asked me to show him Canada and help him to find a job. Having taken him as far as Winnipeg where he took a job as a rodman on a survey for a hydro scheme in Ontario, I returned to Montreal in June 1912 and joined T. Pringle & Sons, consulting engineers.

My first job was as Resident Engineer on the construction of a new factory for Canadian Steel Foundries at Longue Pointe before I was sent to survey the site for a hydro-electric project on the St Maurice river at Grandes-Piles, Quebec. Finally I returned to the Montreal office and worked as a Design Engineer on an 8-storey warehouse for Canadian Fairbanks Morse followed by my appointment as Senior Design Engineer for the reinforced concrete buildings for the new Canadian Kodak factory in Toronto.

When war broke out in Europe in August 1914, I joined the No.5 (Business and Professional Men's) Company of the Westmount Rifles in Montreal. However, seeing no early liklihood of a Second Canadian contingent being sent to France, I decided to return to England and join up there; it seemed the quickest way to complete my training and obtain a commission. I left Canada on 24th December 1914 by train for New York where I paid for my passage to England on the American liner USMS St Louis. So ended my 7 years in Canada.

My experiences in the trenches in the War (1914-1919) are the subject of Volume 3. After the War I spent 4-years in Mesopotamia with the British Army of Occupation as a Lieutenant Colonel in charge of the Mechanical and Electrical Services in Baghdad and Basrah from 1919-1924; those years are covered in Volume 4.

However, before concluding this Volume 2, I have included my two subsequent brief visits to Canada. The first was on my way home from Mesopotamia in 1924 when I arrived in Vancouver on the Empress of Canada after a voyage from Bombay and crossed Canada on the CPR to Montreal, looking up relatives and old friends on the way. The second was in 1964 when, aged 81, I flew to Montreal and joined my son Brian, then 21, when he had finished a vacation job with Canadian Industries Ltd (CIL) in Brownsburg. We travelled across Canada on the CPR, visiting some of the places where I had worked 50 years earlier, and I introduced him to my friends and our relatives in British Columbia.

Harry C. Lott

Emigration and the Adventures
of a Young Engineer in Canada
(1907-1914)

Emigration to Canada – July 1907

My brief visit to Canada on the Atlantic Cable expedition had whetted my appetite and given me a glimpse of life in that young and fast-growing country. Two or three members of the family had already gone there, as well as a few fellow engineers from College. My cousin and good friend, Arthur Barnard, had left for Calgary in 1903, to be followed by his father and sisters after his mother died in 1904 and, in October 1906, my Aunt Agnes emigrated to British Columbia at the age of 42 immediately after her wedding to the 22-year-old groom, Charlie Green, which had caused such a scandal.

And so it was that at 3 pm on 5th July 1907, just two months after I had obtained Father's permission and two weeks before my 24th birthday, I boarded the SS Victorian at Liverpool docks bound for a new life in Canada. My profession on the passenger manifest was shown as Electrical Engineer and my destination as Montreal. Amongst the others on the manifest were fitters, surveyors, engineers, cooks and housewives, all destined for a variety of Canadian cities.

1

S.S. Victorian

The SS Victorian had been built for the Allan Line in 1904 for the North Atlantic run. It was the first large civilian ship propelled by steam turbines and was used during WWI as an armed merchant cruiser for the patrol and protection of the North Atlantic convoys.

My tiny 2nd Class cabin was very crowded, accommodating six of us, together with all our personal belongings in suitcases and portmanteaux, as there was no baggage room for 2nd Class passengers. In those days there was also no forced ventilation and a notice in the cabin stated that the port-hole was not to be opened!

In looking for a seat at table in the dining room I came across M.S. Kennedy, an Associate of the City & Guilds like myself. He was also going to Montreal, Toronto and Winnipeg on a similar errand and we arranged to sit together.

Initially the weather was fine but bitterly cold. A moderate swell on the first day out caused 70% of the passengers, including myself, to go down with seasickness and I spent most of the day

SS Victorian Passenger List

INSTRUCTIONS TO PURSERS.—Each passenger should be given a card indicating the number of sheet and line on sheet his name is to be found on.

	Amount of Cash. To be filled in by Immigration Agent at Port of Landing	NAME OF PASSENGER	Age of Adults			Age to			Profession, Occupation or Calling of Passengers	Nation or Country of Birth			Place of ultimate destination of Passengers excepting "Tourists and returned Canadians, who are to be as described.
		2nd. Cabin for Canada.											
	6520	Louisa Knight	45					M	CARPENTER H. wife	England			Toronto
	425	Percy Kortright	14					S	Engineer				Macleod, Alb.
	9176	Ernst Laband	9					M	Fitter				Hamilton Ont.
		Edith		30					H. wife				
	7953	Frederic Lander	38						Basket maker				Toronto
	2077	Mabel Lea	21						CARPENTER				Hamilton O.t.
	1472	Alfred Leach		HOSPITAL					farming Lady Companion				Winnipeg
	33999	May Leathwood	25						Surveyor				Vancouver B.C.
	0414	Tricey LeMay	3						Rancher				Montreal
	18346	Joseph Lill							Clerk H.S. America				Calgary Alb.
	0473	Harry Lipsett	21							England			Montreal
	1406	Anna Long	21						Recps mill				Toronto
	3197	Mary Longbottomy	31						TRAINED NURSE				Valleyfield
	563	Alice Lord	42					S	Elec. Engr				Brockville Ont.
	18231	Harry Lott	23						Cook Ireland				Montreal
		Kathleen McCarthy	45					M	Motor mechanic				St. John N.B.
	16291	Joseph McGivn	25					S	FARMER IN CAN.	Scotland			Cobourg Ont.
	7332	John McIntyre	49					M	CLERK				Tourist
	0434	William McIntyre	30					S	RET'D CANADIANS	England			Ingersoll Ont.
	861	McLean		RET'D CANADIAN				M	CLERK				RET'D CANADIANS
	0367	Elizabeth Maher	42						Matron				Montreal
	751	Beatrice Maillard	45						none RET'D CANADIANS				Winnipeg
	0088	Maria Malone		RET'D CANADIAN				S	RET'D CANADIANS				RET'D CANADIANS
		Nellie		RET'D CANADIAN				S	FARMING				RET'D CANADIANS
	4558	Margaret Mausell		32					wife	Scotland			Ranfurly Alb.
		Thomas											
	7832	Nellie Markland		TOURIST				S	Teacher TOURIST	England			TOURIST. Tourist
	7051	Walter Markham	43						Clerk				Toronto
	4915	Alennus Marsh	42	TOURIST				M	Chemist TOURIST				TOURIST Tourist
	20323	Lillian "	28						H. wife				Victoria B.C.
		William "	7					S					
	6999	Walter "	32					S	Ironmonger				Winnipeg
	38853	Arthur Marshall	24					M	Joiner				Toronto
	8517	Frank "	37					M	Surveyor				Montreal
	6742	George "						S	Mining bags				Toronto
	841	Joseph "	18						J Brewer				RET'D CANADIAN

3

on my bunk. However, after that the sea was calmer, and I attended the Sunday service at which the Bishops of Quebec and Selkirk (Yukon) officiated. At concerts in the evenings I acted as official piano accompanist to various singers and opened one concert with a Prelude by Rachmaninov.

On the afternoon of July 8th a dense fog developed in the Atlantic which lasted for three days and nights during which time the fog-horn sounded at one-minute intervals and the ship's speed slowed considerably. As we approached Labrador the fog lifted and we found ourselves in the midst of icebergs of all shapes and sizes, 'a glorious sight' in the brilliant sunshine.

There was general excitement as we first sighted land in the Straits of Belle Isle, after which it took us 65 hours to reach Montreal. The passage up the St Lawrence was close to land all the way and full of interest. We passed forests, sawmills, lighthouses, a continuous 'village' of white fishermen's houses and occasional churches, and we were entertained by spouting whales and black and silver porpoises.

The Montreal Gazette summed up the experience well when it said that *"few other things can give a Canadian a keener thrill of pleasure than to come up the St Lawrence in fine summer weather with English friends who are seeing the country for the first time. No other continent has an approach from the sea so noble and impressive. A sense of breadth and space and vast distances dominates everything. As the traveller comes through the narrow Straits of Belle Isle and thinks that his voyage is nearly at an end he learns that ahead of him are as many miles of navigable waters as he has already passed over since leaving Liverpool."*

It is some 700 miles from the ocean to Montreal which we reached on 15th July after 11 days at sea and a brief stop at Quebec City where Kennedy and I went for a walk and had tea at the Chateau Frontenac with its magnificent view over the river before re-joining our ship.

Icebergs on arrival in Canada

Steamers docked in Montreal Harbour - 1910

The Incline Railway up Mount Royal

Arriving in Canada with only £10 in my pocket, I had to make desperate efforts to get a job although our first priority was to find a bed for the night. Kennedy and I went to St Lawrence Hall where we booked a room and then took the Incline Railway to the top of Mount Royal to eat our lunch of some large peaches (40 cents a dozen) and enjoy the view. We then called on two fellow Central Technical College (CTC) graduates, E.G. Sterndale Bennett and H.M. Warner. Warner was about to leave Montreal and recommended we take a room at Mrs MacFarlane's in 51 Victoria Street where he was living, which we did the next day.

From the iceberg temperatures of the North Atlantic we found the 80+ degree July heat and high humidity in the city extremely oppressive and I experienced my first attack of 'prickly heat' which inflamed all the skin's sweat glands.

After visits to several firms without any luck, I met Mr J.C. Rose (of Rose & Laflamme) whose name I had been given by Bernard Collett in Gainsborough. He introduced me to Dr Milton Hersey, a consulting mining engineer working for the City of

Montreal, who had set up a mineral testing laboratory in the city. Dr Hersey became a millionaire from his interests in a silver mining company called Coniagas, named after its mixed orebody containing cobalt (Co), nickel (Ni), silver (Ag) and arsenic (As). He had been a young surveyor at the time and was on the party that discovered the mine in 1903. One of the Timmins brothers who owned the local store had helped to finance the prospect as well as another discovery by Hollinger nearby, with the result that the flourishing mining community which developed there was named after him.

My First Job as an Inspector

Dr Hersey gave me a letter of introduction to Mr Kenny of the Allis Chalmers Bullock Company, electrical plant manufacturers, based in Rockfield near Lachine, and he told me to turn up on Monday morning for an interview. Needing an income immediately, I accepted their offer of 'only 15 cents an hour' and so, seven days after my arrival in Montreal, I was working at Rockfield, 6 miles out of town, in their high-tension testing department. I got the job because I had graduated in electrical engineering and had had 2 years practical experience. Unskilled Italian labourers digging foundations outside were paid a considerably higher rate! It was years before I, a qualified engineer, could earn as much as a good craftsman, carpenter or plasterer, but I had enough to live on.

Life in those early weeks was far from easy; the work was hard and even hazardous as there were none of the most basic safety precautions against electric shock and death from the high tension 2,200 volt apparatus.

The day began with breakfast at 6 am in a nearby café and a walk to catch the 6.30 am train to Rockfield. The 10-hour working day was broken at noon for half-an-hour for a sandwich lunch. Back in Montreal at 6 pm I had my second meal of the day. With the journeys to and from the works adding to the hours, I became more 'fagged out' than I had been with the 11½ hour days of

7

manual work in England. My weight in my clothes was only 12 stone (168 lbs) and I was almost 6ft 2ins.

On Sundays, often with J.W.A (Alec) Miller and Laurence Band, my new friends from work, I went to services and sampled the music and sermons at various churches in the city. Then I would settle down to write my regular letters to Mother, Clara and other members of the family and friends. After more than 3 weeks in Canada, just as I was 'feeling disgusted at the non-arrival of any letters from England', a letter from Father arrived on 10th August. Letters also arrived from James Marshall (Gainsborough) asking my view of the prospects for electrical men in Canada and Jack Musson telling of his departure for Buenos Aires to work on a railway project at £25/month. Warner, who had just arrived back in England, also wrote asking about my success (or otherwise) in getting work.

At Rockfield I quickly became familiar with the connections and methods of testing the insulation and performance of large 1500 kW 11,000 volt alternators and 125 kW motor-generator sets and plotting the saturation and load curves of 100 HP squirrel cage induction motors, but the work was tedious and tiring.

After 6 weeks of this I had an offer of a job in Sydney with the Nova Scotia Steel & Coal Company at $100 per month as a mechanical draughtsman in their steel works. Being shockingly poor on a drawing board and knowing nothing whatever of rolling mill design or operation, I used this offer to look around for another more suitable post. On 4th September, just before I was about to leave for Sydney (NS), I was offered and accepted with much outward hesitation but with inward alacrity, a job at $75 per month, about twice my pay at Rockfield, as an inspector with the Canadian Inspection Company of Montreal. The company was employed by Government departments, railways and corporations to inspect and check steelwork fabrication and erection, electric cables, cement and rolling mill products.

My boss at the Canadian Inspection Co. was a half-educated and often ill-mannered businessman. However, my work, more often than not, satisfied him. As a change from checking steelwork and tapping thousands of rivets at the bridge works I was sent on other jobs such as cement sampling (hot and extremely dirty), testing cables and telephone wires and also railroad ties. In the bridge works I sometimes inspected 80 tons of completed steelwork in a day. One day, working late till 9.30 pm, 'I got on far better when the motley crowd of painters, swarming on our girders almost before we have inspected them, had gone on their way - they include Poles, Italians, Russians and Indians, the last from the Indian village of Caughnawaga across the St Lawrence river.'

Although my new work, again in overalls, was almost as hard in the works of the Dominion Bridge Co at Lachine as it had been at Rockfield, it was more varied. The morning and evening train journey was the same, as were the hours, but at midday I had a good meal at the firm's club house of soup, meat, vegetables, pudding or pie and coffee, all for 16 cents. And I was also impressed by the fact that 'the Managing Director, Phelps Johnson, a man of great wealth, has the same meal with us.'

Like all young men in my position I rented a bedroom in a house where no meals were served. Meals at cafés were good and cheap and I made a deal for 21 meals a week for $3.50. A typical evening meal comprised soup, roast beef with two vegetables, plum pudding with sweet sauce, bread and butter and coffee – with a clean table cloth and quick service. Looking back from today (1966) and with the recent experience of expensive meals during my trip across the country in 1964 with my son, I realise that nearly half a century ago menus were much more varied and interesting.

My 1908 diary records that in a small hotel in New Glasgow, a little Nova Scotian town some 1,000 miles east of Montreal, where the board and lodging charge was only $2.00 a day, Sunday dinner comprised:

Olives

Oxtail soup

Salmon Mayonnaise

Roast turkey with cranberry sauce, compote of fruit, peach
    fritters with beans, potatoes, and tomatoes

Peach pie and jelly

Cheese

Almonds, raisins and apples

Tea

Life in Montreal – 1907/8

At weekends, from mid-day Saturday, I enjoyed the company of a
few friends of my own age. Through Miller and Band I met Harry
Cutmore who had been in the army in South Africa and we
became the best of friends, the three of us often getting together
for dinner or outings. We visited a variety of churches on Sundays,
including Presbyterian, Methodist and Unitarian as well as
Anglican and Catholic in search of a good preacher or good
music. The finest were at Christ Church Cathedral and High
Mass at St James Cathedral where the sermon was in French. The
most famous preacher we heard was the Rev. Dr Paterson Smyth,
whose sermons were, and still are, recognised as classic.

I had been reading 'The Riddle of the Universe' by Prof. Ernst
Haeckel, an eminent biologist who saw the profound impact of
Darwin's theory of evolution on human thought and religion and
extrapolated its principles to the meaning of life, the nature of
reality and the connection between physiology and thought. His
work added fuel to the debate between the religious creationists
and the scientific evolutionists. In a similar vein I had also been
reading a book by Dr Thomas Hudson, a leading authority on
metaphysics, called 'The Laws of Psychic Phenomena' in which he
formulated natural laws relating to the mind in the same way that
Newton established the mechanical laws of nature.

At the Fraser Library I exchanged these books for Grant Allen's 'Colours of Flowers' and Huxley's 'Science and Culture'. Thomas Henry Huxley FRS was known as Darwin's Bulldog for his famous support of Darwin's theory of evolution. His work, together with those of others I had been reading, led to my becoming what I called a 'Christian Agnostic', an agnostic but with Christian values and morality.

On rare occasions I enjoyed hospitality in private houses or flats. In one flat, that of Prof. Cox, MA (Cantab), PhD and Mrs Cox, we demonstrated the dryness of the atmosphere in winter by lighting a gas jet with a spark from a finger after rubbing our shoes on a rug to generate a static electric charge. Incidentally, all house lighting was by gas and I used a gas jet in my room to make a cup of tea or cocoa in a small saucepan held over the flame.

In October, before the freeze-up, heavy rain turned the city streets and sidewalks into an 'awful state' making the place 'not worth living in', or so I wrote at the time. On 26th November, with the arrival of snow, the 'jingling of the sleigh bells took the place of the rattling of the iron-tired wheels on the rough cobblestones'.

In December, Miller, Band, Cutmore and I started a debating club as part of a self-improvement scheme for public speaking, using as our first topic 'How best to overcome the drink curse!' Wellard and Stacey joined in and the following week I prepared a paper for our next debate on the motion 'Athletics are overdone'.

About this time I moved downstairs in the rooming house to a more expensive lower front room paying $12.00 a month, $2 more for the better accommodation.

It was in Montreal that I had my first demonstration of the innate and absolute honesty of the Chinese residents, all laundrymen, a reputation which I understand that race still had in the country when I returned for a visit some 57 years later. A Chinaman would knock on the door of a rooming house; the landlady, knowing his business but knowing absolutely nothing about the man, would let him in and, alone, he would go into the rooms occupied by the lodgers to deliver clean linen and collect payment for it. If the lodger was not at home he would leave the parcel and trust his client to pay on his next visit. Having completed his business in the house he let himself out. They always replaced any articles lost in the wash. Who, of any other country, would have been given such privilege?

When winter came I had difficulty in getting skating boots large enough, for my foot was about 12 inches long – apparently not many are! We English immigrants, having been accustomed to skate on comparatively thin ice that flexed, were the first to venture out onto the ice on the rivers and lakes where we had some wonderfully exciting outings. By the time most Canadians considered the ice thick enough, snow had fallen and made that type of skating impossible for the rest of the winter. We then went several times a week to the Victoria Ice Rink where we met friends and sometimes skated for two or three hours at a time.

On December 17th I learnt of the death of Lord Kelvin. I had shaken hands with him six months earlier at a Conversazione of the Institution of Electrical Engineers in London and had seen him at the Engineering Conference the next day when the Hon. C.A. Parsons read a paper on 'Turbines for Marine Propulsion'.

Christmas Day was the only day we had off work and I changed into knickerbockers and sweater and went snowshoeing with friends. We had just bought the snowshoes which were 14 inches wide and 3ft 6in long and cost $2.50 each, including the long laces of lamp-wick.

Winter in Montreal

Christmas Day 1907 - snowshoeing with friends.

After a heavy fall of snow – Montreal 1907

My First Winter in Canada - January 1908

In early January I met up at 8 pm on a Friday evening with Laurence Band and other members of the Zingari Snow-shoe Club for a tramp over Mount Royal, across the Park Slide lit up with arcs and thronged with tobogganers, and on to Côte des Neiges to Lumkins Hotel where we had a drink and watched the gambling on the roulette tables before returning home at 11.30 pm. Evening snow-shoe tramps with the Zingari Club became one of our regular 'winter sports' involving up to 15 of us Englishmen and a similar number of Canadian girls.

Tobogganing on the Park Slide was so popular that there was a long waiting list for membership. The slide was a run of about ½ mile long straight down the slope of the mountain, well lighted with electric arc lights. I was lucky to be friendly with a member and had a thrilling experience on my first evening. The flat toboggans, on lignum vitae or bone runners, were started at the top with a push off by one of the crew. There were 4 parallel grooves, so that 4 toboggans could go down in a race together. I believe that the best runs took about ½ a minute so that, allowing for the gradual slowing down to a halt at the bottom, a maximum speed of perhaps 100 miles per hour could have been reached on the upper, steeper slope. I went down with my friend and his fiancée. For the first run I was put in front, his fiancée stretched on me, her head behind mind and my friend on her with the maximum of 'overlap' for the toboggan was only 8 feet long. After the first run or two, it was suggested that I should take the rear position. Whether my friend did not lie as far forward as possible, or whether it was my long body, I could not lie flat enough and, with my knees on the tail end of the toboggan, my centre of gravity and my back and backside were too high. The result was that, after oscillating sideways in the groove, we suddenly overturned. Clinging together and to the toboggan, we went down the steepest part of the slope upside down. Spectators alongside the tracks rushed up as we slowed down, expecting to find casualties but, except for bruised shoulders and egos, we were unhurt. After that, my friend, to reassure his girlfriend and me, took us down again separately. The steep climb back up the hill after the run kept us warm even in below zero weather.

By the end of January ten feet of snow had fallen in Montreal and in early February several of us contracted 'la grippe, a fever which left me weak, shivering and shaking like an old man!' Inhaling Friars Balsam antiseptic vapour to relieve nasal congestion was the only treatment available. With strong winds and brilliant blue skies, the temperature in the city fell to -24 degrees (all temperatures are in Fahrenheit) at night and only rose to -10 degrees during the day. I narrowly escaped frost bite returning from work one Saturday on the crowded gangway of a street-car during a blizzard, completely covered with 2-3 inches of snow.

On 18th February, Band, Miller and I went to the Park Slide again to join 20,000 people at the annual 'Fête de Nuit'. Electric illuminations, rockets, Roman candles and coloured flares created a strange and beautiful scene against the clear night sky whilst 2,000 people used the Club's six slides. On returning to my room I made myself a cocoa and whipped cream before turning in!

The Park Slide – Montreal

Canadian Sport Series.   Waltzing on skates.

Waltzing on an Ice Rink in Montreal c.1908

Winter scene on the slopes of Mount Royal

Our other winter sport was ice-skating, and the Victoria Ice Rink was a regular evening venue where many of us met up after supper. Band and I generally skated together and were often joined by the Misses Walker and Miss May Farbrother whom we accompanied on circuits of the rink. The season ended and the rink closed in mid-March when sleighs were gradually disappearing from the streets and wheeled vehicles taking their place.

During extremely cold weather the cream on the top of the milk bottles left on the front doorstep by the milkman would freeze and expand upwards so that if you were late in collecting your milk on Sunday mornings you were liable to have lost the cream; dogs could be seen going from door to door removing the cardboard cover and enjoying a breakfast of ice-cream.

Canada was a popular destination for engineering graduates from the Central Technical College and there were a number of us in Montreal. With E.G. Sterndale Bennett and C.G.J. Luck I helped to organise a dinner for the Old Students at the impressive CPR railway hotel, Place Viger. There were 18 of us present; J.W. Hayward took the chair and I proposed the toast to 'The Guests', accompanying songs on the piano afterwards.

Old Central Technical College Students' dinner -
I am tallest in the back row

Sterndale Bennett and McHaffie were also the prime movers of a
group of us who began to meet in the evenings to discuss the idea
of forming a contractors' company for prospecting in the West.
However, after attending two or three meetings I decided to
withdraw. Letters from Jack Musson in Buenos Aires had made
me consider going to South America and I signed up for some
Spanish lessons with Cutmore whom I regularly joined for supper
at the Regal café.

For musical entertainment we attended organ recitals at the
Church of the Messiah (25c.), a concert by the celebrated pianist
Vladimir de Pachmann (75c. back seat), and a performance of
Carmen at His Majesty's Theatre followed a few days later by
Gounod's Faust. In order to keep up my own key-board skills I
applied for spare-time appointments as organist at St Andrews
church, Westmount, and at the Church of the Messiah. However,
it was fortunate that I didn't succeed in either case for, in April

1908, I was sent to New Glasgow, Nova Scotia, on an inspection job away from the city.

My diary records the result of a visit to Prof. A. Young, a phrenologist and palmist, who examined me, measured my cranium and concluded that 'I was of mental temperament and must cultivate a large amount of vital force to support the extraordinarily large brain!' He said 'I lacked destructiveness (executiveness) and combativeness', a diagnosis which left a deep impression on me and remained with me for the rest of my life.

I went down with a heavy cold, a terrible throat and high temperature and was confined to bed by the doctor for a week, upsetting the plans of my boss J.S. Griffiths to send me to Winnipeg. However, a few days after returning to work, I was told to 'be prepared to leave for Nova Scotia tonight'! After tidying up things at work and packing, the next morning I went to the city office for final instructions before catching the Maritime Express I.C.R. leaving Bonaventure for Nova Scotia at noon on 9th April.

New Glasgow, Nova Scotia - Inspector on Bridge Works – April 1908

It was a brilliantly clear cold day and the trees looked wonderful, sparkling with icicles. We crossed the St Lawrence, about half water and half ice, on the Victoria Jubilee Bridge and reached New Glasgow late the following evening after a journey of 34½ hours. I put up at the Norfolk House, a very decent hotel, for $2 a day inclusive, and stayed there for two nights before moving to Mrs Cooke's 'Cooke House' for $5 a week board and lodging.

The next morning I reported to our senior inspector, H.P. Moore, at the rolling mills of the Nova Scotia Steel & Coal Company in Trenton. He seemed pleased to see me arrive to help him with the bridge inspection. I collected the drawings and specifications from Moore and walked up the hill to McNeil & Co's bridge works to meet the draughtsman and walk around the fabrication shop.

I had no idea how difficult the month I was to spend there would be; the small workshop was not properly equipped, nor capable of fabricating to a reasonable specification the pin-connected truss bridge designed to span 176 ft.

After some terrible wordy conflicts with Mr Charles McNeil, eventually I had my way, insisting on having 16 plates, with 8 rivets each, cut off and replaced. My rejection of these and other riveted plates caused the irate McNeil to appeal to our client, the Government of New Brunswick, to have me removed, but my Montreal boss upheld my decision. Despite their support, I had many more unpleasant encounters in the works before I got satis-factory steelwork provided.

I never saw the bridge after it was erected, and so I did not learn if my inspections had been sufficiently thorough. If I had not been so severe the bridge would probably have sagged instead of having the usual camber in the middle of the span!

Sundays in the small town were quiet and I attended both the morning and evening services at St George's Church as well as some weekday evening services, playing the organ and accompa-nying the choir at their practices. Music was my form of relaxa-tion and at Hamilton's store I listened to their gramophone and bought some organ music.

Walks with colleagues up Fraser's Mountain, along the East River and to the Sutherland's River and Park's Falls kept me reasonably fit. One evening we walked to the Acadia Coal Mine which was producing 400-500 tons/day of some of the best coal in the country but was being worked dangerously close to the Old Forge Pit which had flooded with water after a fire and contained the bodies of 75 men.

During my work on the road bridge fabrication I had the good fortune to be coached in rolling mill inspection by Moore and I used, as usual, the inspector's "CI" hammer to mark all accepted steel sections. This hammer was subsequently stolen and used by the Rolling Mill Company to mark steel that they knew would be rejected by our resident inspector at the mills. Later in Montreal I was able to confirm that some of this steel, sold to the Dominion Bridge Co., was never inspected or accepted by us - sharp practice at the Rolling Mill Co which did not pay off.

On 9th May, my work at Trenton completed, I said goodbye to Moore, McNeil and the others and caught the train to Truro where I changed into a Parlour Car of the Maritime Express bound for Montreal.

Quebec Bridge Collapse – 1907

My inspection of the New Glasgow bridge steelwork and the riveting had been particularly rigorous, partly as a result of lessons learned from the disastrous collapse of the Quebec Bridge during its construction a few months earlier in August 1907, with the loss of 86 lives.

The Quebec Bridge had been designed to be the longest bridge in the world and to outstrip the reputation of the bridge over the Firth of Forth. The cantilever design had been selected as the 'best and cheapest' solution by Theodore Cooper, the rather proud and arrogant American consulting engineer responsible for the design. He had written in an American Engineering Society paper in 1891:

"You all know about the Firth of Forth bridge – the clumsiest structure ever designed by man, the most awkward piece of engineering, in my opinion, that was ever constructed from the American point of view. An American would have taken that bridge with the amount of money that was appropriated and would have turned back 50% to the owners instead of collecting, when the bridge was done, nearly 40% in excess of the estimate."

Following the disaster, a newspaper quoted this comment by Cooper and concluded:

September 1907 – Firth of Forth bridge is UP
September 1907 – Quebec (American) bridge is DOWN!

During the construction of the bridge the Canadian inspecting engineers noticed that some of the lower steel members had started to buckle and, although this had been reported to the designer, he had refused to listen to the 'inferior opinions' of the local engineers.

The collapsed Quebec Bridge in 1907

After the collapse, Canadian Government engineers took over the design using 'heavier and uglier' cantilever arms and the bridge was completed in 1917, but not before another disaster occurred in 1916 when the centre span fell whilst being hoisted into place, killing 13.

Return to Montreal – May to August 1908

On arrival back in Montreal I reported to Griffiths at the Canadian Inspection Company's new offices in the Canadian Express Building on McGill Street. He told me 'to get a room in Montreal for a time' and sent me out to the Lakefield Cement Works at Pointes-aux-Trembles, an hour's run by street car from the city, to sample car loads of cement for the National Transcontinental Railway Company. After taking the samples and sealing the cars I sent the samples to our office for testing and spent a couple of evenings at the Canadian Society of Civil Engineers library to read up on cement. One awful morning, after sealing 160 bags of cement, I left with my nose and throat filled with setting cement and clothes thick with its dust. My days of sampling cement, including 8000 bags of Condor (Belgian) Portland Cement, were fortunately intermixed with days back at the Dominion Bridge Co. on inspections and tensile testing (in a Riehle machine) the steelwork for the Harbour Shed and New Post Office and as well as testing hard drawn copper telephone wire at the Wire & Cable Works.

I had been bunking down in Miller's and Cutmore's rooms for a few days before finding new digs at 50 Mackay Street. When Miller left, I moved into his room at 159 Stanley Street after being 'interviewed' by the landlady, Mrs Duncan.

The days were getting warmer and the temperature on Empire Day (25th May) rose to 69 degrees F. It was a public holiday and I spent the evening with Mrs and Miss Rose, Miss McCord, Gilden and McNeil. 'We sat upstairs on the veranda and watched the fireworks and a wonderful display of the Aurora Borealis with its waves of light shimmering as if blown about by a fan. It continued from 8 pm until midnight when I walked home after some supper and music.'

Most mornings I went to the Regal Café for breakfast with Harry Cutmore at 6.15 am and we sometimes had supper there also. When not with Cutmore, I liked to meet up with Laurence Band and Wellard for supper in the café at the Strathcona Hotel.

A few days in the Laurentians

In June I was sent to Shawbridge, not far from St Agathe in the Laurentians, to inspect the painting of three railroad bridges on the Canadian Northern Railway line between Shawbridge and St Jerome. My lodgings were at John Boyd's general store where I had meals with him and his family; he had the contract to carry out the work using a patented paint called Wasatch. Shawbridge was one of the few English villages in Quebec and a favourite summer weekend resort for Montrealers.

It was the softest inspection job I had had - I could sit on the grass and write letters when not watching the painting - but it did not last long. After a few days I received an instruction from Griffiths to transfer to a bridge erection job over the St Anne's River and so I left by train from St Jerome via Three Rivers to the little French village of La Chevrotière, where hardly anyone could speak more than a few words of English.

Bridge Inspection at St Casimir

On arrival I met Griffon, the boss of the contractors O'Brien and Mullarky, and we walked 6 miles along the newly laid track to St Casimir, 160 miles east of Montreal, where the bridge was being erected for the Canadian Northern Railway. The day was extremely hot, and mosquitoes made life almost unbearable.

It was during my work at St Casimir that the most serious protest against my inspection came from a French-Canadian riveter working on the plate-girder bridge of four 90 ft spans. I marked two or three rivets in an inside corner to be cut out and replaced. It is possible that the rivets were a second and serious attempt to get a good-looking head on each, so my yellow rings around them raised the ire of the riveter who came after me with a sledge hammer! If he had knocked me off my balance, for I had to cross from one side of the bridge to the other on diagonals only 6 inches wide, he could have been acquitted of murder as I could easily have slipped and fallen onto the rocks below. But murder he felt like committing at that moment. I told the foreman of the incident and said that either the riveter or I would have to leave the job, and that I intended to stay. How the affair ended I am not sure, although my diary says 'of course I got my way'! Probably the new rivets driven in this awkward inside corner were no better than those that I had marked.

The transport of those eight 90 ft plate girders from La Chevrotière to the bridge site at St Casimir also proved a headache for me. The 6 miles of un-ballasted railroad track from the main line was over swamps and through woods. It had to remain un-ballasted until the new bridge gave access to the ballast pits beyond. I was very doubtful if the girders, about 10 ft deep and standing that height above the flat-bed rail wagons, would not tip over on the soft and uneven track. I calculated how much they could be tilted without falling over and was able to satisfy myself that if the locomotive went very slowly, so that there was no rocking motion, there was a reasonable margin of safety.

I myself rode on the cow-catcher of the engine, so that if it rolled over onto its side in the soft ground, I could jump clear on the other side! I did not feel responsible for the safety of the locomotive.

St Casimir was another small French-Canadian village where no-one except the Chinese laundryman could speak much English. I shall never forget my journey from there back to Montreal. It involved a ride of a few miles to the station at night in absolute darkness in a horse-drawn rig; frightening because the driver kept falling asleep, despite my frequent prods. I couldn't even tell if the horse was keeping to the rough road and I didn't know the way. But with my usual luck, I was in time to catch the midnight train to Three Rivers, a town of 12,500 people where a major fire had burned down part of the town only a few days before. There I changed to the Montreal train, reached the city at 7 am and went straight to my room.

Montreal - July 1908

Back in the office the next day Griffiths told me that in August he wanted me to go to Winnipeg to inspect the erection of the great Union Station and to get further inspection work in the district. In other words, he was asking me to start a new branch of the Canadian Inspection Company there whilst carrying out the inspection job. In the meantime, I was to continue inspecting and testing steel at the Structural Steel Co.'s works in Montreal. At least I was able

Harry Lott aged 25 in 1908

to enjoy excellent lunches at the nearby Maples Hotel where a typical lunch, costing 25 cents, included kidney soup, fricassee of turkey and rice with apple fritters, beans and potatoes, chicken salad, raisin pie and water ice with lemonade or coffee.

Another of my jobs involved testing rubber covered telephone wire at the Wire & Cable Co. and, at the end of the month, I had to go back to St Casimir for a further week's inspection work on the bridge, standing in for Crutchley whose father had just had a fatal accident.

Mr and Mrs Rose occasionally invited me for supper at their home on Metcalfe Avenue, Westmount, where we were sometimes joined by Mrs and Miss McCord and Mr Gilden. In these relatively rare visits to private homes as an evening guest, I found that my ability to entertain people by playing the piano was particularly useful. I had learnt a few humorous musical sketches, a form of humour at the piano which today seems missing from TV programmes; Victor Borge being perhaps the last of that genre.

Holidays were confined to the very few public holidays. On Dominion Day (July 1st) a few friends and I boarded an over-crowded steamer at Lachine for a 53 mile trip up the St Lawrence and Ottawa rivers, through the Lake of the Two Mountains, past St Anne de Bellevue, Como, Oka (an Indian village) and Rigaud to Carillon at the foot of the Ottawa river rapids, returning down the Lachine rapids. The river trip provided some relief from the oppressive heat of the city where downtown temperatures rose to 96 degrees, the highest for seven years. The previous Sunday we had taken the steamer Chateaugay on a trip up the St Lawrence, between the islands and back down the Lachine Rapids where the standing waves resembled Atlantic rollers.

On 6th July the papers were full of aeroplane records. 'Farnham's plane kept up for 19 minutes and Count Zeppelin's airship or diri-gible balloon, 425 feet long and carrying 15 passengers, was suc-cessful in Germany.' Other events I recorded included a procession in Quebec in front of the Prince of Wales and Lord Roberts on 23rd July to celebrate the tercentenary of Champlain's founding of the city, and a couple of days later, the winner of the Marathon at the Olympic Games in London. Laurence Band and I discussed these and other topical issues, such as a House of Lords debate on 'the India Question', during our regular evenings together, whilst Miller was busy developing and printing our photos.

Having spent my first Montreal winter without an overcoat, I felt that my thick English blood was thinning. I had saved a little money and was able to buy a long black overcoat with a deep

Persian Lamb collar for $40.00. It went well with my new Persian lamb cap (still in good condition today) which I wore when travelling through Russia and Siberia in below zero weather in 1929 and also in recent years when skating in England.

Montreal – circa 1908

St Lawrence Street

Sherbrooke Street (above)

St James Street (right)

Winnipeg, Manitoba - 1908

On 15th August, a month after my 25th birthday, I was told to leave for Winnipeg by the evening train! I went to the Dominion Bridge Company to pick up the drawings and was given final instructions by Griffiths with a letter of introduction to Col. Ruttan MICE, the City of Winnipeg Chief Engineer, to whom I was to report. Before leaving Montreal I spent a couple of evenings in the library of the Canadian Society of Civil Engineers studying the theory of bridge design, and especially swing spans, so that I was well prepared.

Band, Miller, Stacey and Wellard saw me off on the Pacific Express which left Montreal at 10.30 pm. Cutmore had called to say goodbye earlier. The fare for the 1,450 mile journey was $35, plus $8 for a sleeping berth and $4.75 for excess baggage. During the two day journey I made the acquaintance of two English ladies; one a young grandmother on a world tour and the other, younger, returning from Japan. It was their first experience of being in a sleeping car with a man, and in an upper berth!

Within hours of arrival in Winnipeg I had reported to Wilson, Ruttan's Assistant Chief Engineer, met E.E. Shephard of the Dominion Bridge Co. and started my inspection of the bridge. It was a through-truss steel road bridge which had an electrically operated central swing span and crossed the Red River at Redwood Avenue.

I had taken a room at the Queen's Hotel for the first two nights before moving, on Cunningham's advice, to a rather pokey room at 221 Edmonton Street for $9/month. Meals were not provided and so I paid $4 for a 21-meal ticket at a boarding house on York Avenue where 'the meals were substantial, but the service was without style' but, more importantly, there was a piano. Unfortunately, my old complaint of nasal catarrh with a sore throat recurred and I treated it with glycothylamine so that it did not stop me working.

Close to the bridge site, on the riverbank was an old semi-derelict stable which had belonged to the Hudson Bay Company. In it I discovered a number of ancient account books of the company, showing what they paid Indians for skins (mink, otter and even buffalo) brought in from the prairies and the bush, and also what they charged the Indians for supplies of food. I am afraid that these, almost historic papers, did not receive the care they deserved.

Two months later, a young engineer came from Montreal to assist me in the inspection of steelwork erection for the new Union Railway Station for which we were contracted by the New York firm of architects who had designed it.

The GTP Union Station, Winnipeg

The bridge across the Red River at Redwood Avenue, Winnipeg, when I arrived

The Redwood Avenue Bridge nearing completion (above)
and completed (below)

Their resident architect once asked me an awkward question. Since the extreme range of temperatures in Winnipeg was 140 degrees, the 360 ft long steel bridge structure would be 3 inches longer above ground on the hottest day (100 deg.) than on the coldest day (-40 deg.), a temperature which actually occurred on 6th January 1909, a few months later. The outside steel columns would therefore never be plumb except at one temperature. I had to think quickly and explained that before the columns were encased in concrete or stone I would make sure that they would be vertical at about 50 degrees. The answer was apparently satisfactory.

Below zero weather and the freeze-up began on 9th November and, although the ice did not reach both banks in all places, a few

of us Englishmen ventured onto the ice and skated on the Assiniboine and Red Rivers which meet at Winnipeg.

On one occasion we each carried a pole for safety in case the ice broke beneath us and in places we had to skirt the riverbank on a shelf of ice only 12 inches wide with open water across

Under the Redwood Avenue Bridge, Winnipeg

the river.

Later we found an ice-rink above Maryland Bridge where we had fast and furious skating in shirt sleeves, however, my attempts to waltz on the ice were not entirely successful and I quickly became dizzy.

In September I moved to a nicer room at 219 Gary Street for which I paid $11/month, well worth the extra $2, and my evening routine became similar to that in Montreal. After work I would have 'supper' (a high tea or early dinner) at about 6 pm at the café at 263 York Avenue where we often had some music and I played my repertoire of songs. I would then return to my room to write my daily report to Ruttan and Griffiths as well as read and write letters to the 'Homeones' and old friends. After that I met up with friends and we would talk or look at photos in one of our rooms or go for a long walk around the city and occasionally call in at the Carnegie Library to borrow a couple more books. My most regular companion was Alex Gray, just as it had been Laurence Band in Montreal and George Borns in Gainsborough, and often Pearson joined us. We talked about our ambitions and ideals and discussed our religious beliefs as well as topical events, generally ending up at the Olympia Café at about 10.30 pm for a 'late supper' of hot buckwheat cakes and maple syrup or an ice-cream sundae before turning in.

I kept up my piano playing whenever I could after breakfast and supper at 263 York Avenue and at occasional private events arranged by Mr & Mrs Swindell and Mr and Miss Deakin whose songs I accompanied. Our only other cultural outings were occasional visits to the Winnipeg Theatre where we saw 'The Wizard of the Nile', 'The Pirates of Penzance' and 'Geisha' amongst others. The performances were often mediocre, and I described one performance at the Unique Theatre as 'a rotten low show'.

On Sundays I maintained my habit of attending a service at one of the city churches and recorded in my diary my opinion of them: St Luke's, Fort Rouge ('a poor service'); Holy Trinity ('service and sermon dry'); All Saints, Broadway ('a very dull service', but on another occasion 'enjoy a good service'); St Michael and All Angels ('an exceedingly high service in a small wooden shack of a church')!

There were of course many times when I retired to my room to laze and read; my choice of books still focused on philosophy, science and religion. I read 'The Saint' by Antonio Fogazzaro whose works reflected the conflict between reason and faith and were condemned by the Vatican; and 'Success among Nations' by Dr Emil Reich, an eminent Hungarian Jew who lectured in Oxbridge on the lessons which history had for the future.

The erection of the bridge went well, and the swing span was in place by Christmas. My visit to the Public Works Department to follow up a contract to inspect new locks at St Andrews probably won me my next job. In Winnipeg my salary had increased by $10 to $85/month, out of which I was generally able to save $20, although clothes and doctor's bills sometimes added $30 to my regular monthly expenses of $50. Nevertheless, I was able to build up a credit balance of about $300 (approx. £60) by the end of the year.

A really cold spell began at the end of November with temperatures of -10 deg. falling to -22 deg. on some nights. On Xmas Eve, Pearson, Gray and I attended midnight Mass at St Mary's Church and heard Gounod's Messe Solonelle. After early communion on Christmas Day, we spent the morning skating. I missed Mrs Mac's big meal at York Avenue and instead went to Paul Schioler's for tea - he was one of the City Engineers I had got to know and who encouraged me to better my position financially.

On 5th January an unexpected telegram from my head office in Montreal read "Leave today if possible for Toronto". So, once again with only 24 hours' notice, I left the next day to a new job in another Province. The following morning, 6th January, the Winnipeg papers reported that *"yesterday and last night were easily the coldest of the present winter. During the day the thermometer registered 30 degrees below zero, but overnight the mercury fell and reached 40 below by the morning. The streets were practically deserted and the few pedestrians who did appear took it on the run with furs bundled closely about them. There were innumerable cases of frozen ears, noses, cheeks and fingers. A white mist clouded the atmosphere at midnight and frost coated everything."*

I was up early to start packing, had breakfast with Pearson and went to the City Engineers office to say goodbye to Schioler, Ruttan and Wilson. After lunching with Alex Gray and a visit to the barber I finished my packing and went to 263 York Avenue for supper and to say goodbye to 'the boys'. Pearson and Gray accompanied me to the station where I caught the 11.00 pm train to Toronto.

Toronto, Ontario - 1909

The 1,230 mile train journey to Toronto took 47 hours; it was relaxing and enjoyable and, like my earlier journeys, provided me with the only holidays I had during my first 18 months in Canada.

My job in Toronto was Chief Inspector for the manufacture, in the workshops of the Canada Foundry Company, of a bridge and movable dam to be erected across the Red River below Winnipeg at St Andrew's Rapids, for the Government of Canada.

The total weight of steelwork and machinery was about 3,000 tons and the Government specifications were extremely severe. The 'Caméré' curtain design of dam was unique on the American continent and was copied, far too slavishly, from a dam in France.

MOVABLE DAM (CAMERÉ CURTAIN TYPE) AT ST ANDREWS RAPIDS, ON THE RED RIVER, BELOW WINNIPEG (MANITOBA)

The purpose of the dam was to raise the level of the Red River by 14ft during the summer navigation season and to blot out the rapids for some miles upstream. Then, when the freeze-up started and navigation had to cease, the dam was raised clear and the river fell to its normal level, except for a permanent 7 ft high concrete weir at the base. The top of the double-deck bridge was for road traffic across the river. The underside of the top deck and the whole space between the two decks were for an overhead travelling crane and winches, all electrically operated. From the underside of the bridge the crane lowered long girders, framed two and four together, hinged at the top and with the lower 'heel' pressing against shoes of cast iron in the weir. Down the upstream face of the girder frames were then unrolled blinds of wooden slats of Southern yellow pine secured at the ends to an endless chain of phosphor bronze links and gun-metal pins which had to be machined to extreme accuracy.

When navigation ceased the blinds were first rolled up and stored between the decks and then the girder frames were raised to a horizontal position under the bridge. The wooden slats were of varying thickness according to their depth below the final water surface.

In this new assignment I had three engineers to assist me – George Milne, Pomfret and A.L.G. (Leonard) Taylor. For me it was a promotion without any increase in salary! One of my assistants was responsible for detailed checking of the bridge

One section of steel dam, with roller curtain, assembled for trial in shops at Toronto. Ont.

A roller curtain assembled for testing

members, the second for the girder frames and the third for all the machinery, whilst I supervised and helped all three.

The difficulty of getting the extreme accuracy demanded by the specification resulted in almost continuous trouble for me with the Canada Foundry Company engineers and I came under fire from my boss. My position eventually became very difficult and my peace of mind was not restored by a measly increase in pay of $5.00 to $90.00 per month.

The upstream side of the completed bridge

I therefore felt inclined to resign when, 3 months after the start of the work Griffiths, my boss from Montreal, came and 'raised hell'. When my firm's local branch manager, Mr L.J. Street, who had been very civil to me on my arrival in Toronto and to whom I had reported almost daily, did not support me and followed Griffith's example, it was the last straw; I threw my hand in and gave him my letter of resignation. He and Griffiths asked me to reconsider, but I demanded such a large increase in pay, to $125 per month, that I felt sure it would not be accepted. They did, however, offer me the 'bait' of a position as 'Representative out West'. This was quite tempting as I would have enjoyed returning to Winnipeg, but I decided to call it a day and left Toronto after 4½ months.

During my first three months in Toronto I had often been extremely lonely, not having found any bachelor friends of my own age with whom to spend evenings and weekends. I generally lunched with Milne, Pomfret or Taylor from the works, but in the evenings I got into very lazy habits, reading and napping in my room after supper and not feeling inclined to go out for walks alone. Fortunately, Mrs Gould, the landlady of the boarding house at 693 Spadina Avenue where I had taken a room, was happy for me to play on the old Broadwood Grand Piano in her drawing room where I often accompanied her 14-year-old daughter Mabel in some songs.

During the evenings I wrote many letters home, to old friends and to several former bosses whom I asked to be referees and support my application for Associate Membership of the Institution of Civil Engineers. Sundays usually began with Choral Celebration at St Thomas Church, Washington Avenue; it was just round the corner from my digs and there was 'unusually fine music by the small choir'. Occasionally I attended a service at St James Cathedral and heard 'an excellent sermon'.

Ice-yachting on Toronto Bay (Lake Ontario)

Laurence Band came from Montreal to spend a few days with me in mid-February and we went ice-yachting on Toronto Bay. I had recently bought a 3A Kodak pocket camera and we took several snaps of each other on the ice and later in High Park where we watched tobogganing, skating and curling.

Sailing on ice at 40 miles per hour

Ice-yachting on Toronto Bay, Lake Ontario – Feb 1909

Feb 13. 09

Feb 28. 09

My diary records our trip to Niagara that Sunday: 'A blizzard - stinging ice-crystals most of the day. After breakfast Band and I catch the train to Niagara Falls; reach there at 11.15 am. Meet J.W.A Miller at the station and we three spend the day together

39

walking round and doing the sites. Unique sight of American Falls – first time so low since 1848 – an ice-jam at the head of the Niagara River caused the American Falls to run dry.'

'The weather conditions are terrible and spoil photography & pleasure. Meals at La Fayette Hotel. Walk right round Goat Island. Walk back to the station & return by train alone. Band and Miller, who see me off, are going to Buffalo for the night. Reach Toronto at 10.20 pm.'

The American Falls during the ice-jam on the Niagara River – 14th February 1909

The ice-jam eventually built up for 12 miles and caused the Niagara River upstream of the Falls to rise 50-60 ft above its normal summer level. Attempts to dynamite it were only partially successful and it did not break up until the end of April.

I went back to Montreal for Easter weekend and met up with Cutmore, Band, Stacey and the others. The Rose's invited me for supper on both the Saturday and Easter Sunday. Miss Rose was there this time and we went for a long walk around Westmount talking about her engagement to Bernard Collett, my old friend from Gainsborough, who had introduced me to her family in 1907 when I first arrived in Canada.

Besides some unexpected hospitality from Dr Thorburn, a Toronto ear specialist whom I had consulted professionally about a spell of severe ear ache and deafness, I was invited to dinner from time to time at 391 Ontario Street by Leonard Taylor and his wife with their 5 year-old son Conrad who years later became a good friend; he retired to Bermuda and died in 1970. Leonard was an Englishman who had been travelling the world as a marine engineer and had had a rough start in Canada. He and his wife sometimes joined me for an evening's skating on Grenadiers Pond; he was a novice but she was a fair skater. I repaid their hospitality with an evening at the Prince's Theatre, where we saw Louis James in Peer Gynt, and afterwards went to 'a little supper at MacConkey's'.

In March the newspapers reported that *'England is in a state of semi-panic owing to the speed with which Germany is building up a Navy. England wants 8 Dreadnought battleships, now supposed to be the latest type, but Canada is slow in offering to help'*.

A month later the Taylors invited me back to the Prince's Theatre to see a performance of 'An Englishman's Home'; the London production had recently given a tremendous boost to the recruitment for the Territorial Army in England. During my last week in Toronto, I paid 25 cents for a seat at the first Popular Concert given by the Toronto Symphony Orchestra in the famous Massey Hall in front of an audience of 3,420, and two or three of us also went to the Island to see a Baseball game between Toronto and Jersey City.

The day before I left I made another visit to Niagara, this time with Leonard Taylor on the steamer the SS Corona, on its very first trip of the season when the peach trees were in full bloom. On that occasion we had to walk ashore from the steamer over the remains of the ice-jam which had carried away the usual landing stages at Lewiston and Queenston. We re-boarded the ship and returned to Toronto that evening where I packed up my things ready to depart the next day on my 'all-the-way-by-water' journey home from Niagara to Liverpool.

The SS Corona alongside the remains of the ice jam

Visit to England – May to August 1909

After saying goodbye to everyone on 18th May, I went to the Imperial Bank to withdraw my savings; a bank draft for $220 and $26 in cash. I had booked a berth on the SS Belleville, a steamer of the R & O Navigation Co. bound for Montreal and the Taylor family came to see me off. As soon as the ship sailed at 9.30 pm I turned in for the night.

The weather was so good that I got sunburnt as we passed the Thousand Islands and went through the Cornwell and Soulanges canals and the Lachine locks. We docked in Montreal early on Friday morning 21st May and I had just enough time to visit the office, have lunch with Band and a few hours with the Roses before going back to the docks and boarding the S.S. Dominion, a cattle boat converted into a comfortable liner of 9,000 tons, for the journey home. By coincidence, the other man in my cabin was the brother of the chief warder of Dorchester gaol, whom of course I did not know!

As we approached the ocean south of Newfoundland, we passed several icebergs and the rough sea caused most of us to retire to our cabins suffering badly from seasickness. It was two or three days before I could enjoy the meals on board and life returned to normal with entertainment after dinner. The ship's doctor, Dr V.P.O. Logan, a young freshly fledged Liverpudlian, organised a concert one evening at which I was asked to be the official accompanist. After that, at the request of several passengers, I accompanied Ethel Lenore Gnaedinger, who sang songs for us such as 'The Rosary', 'Abide with Me' and 'Indian Love Lyrics'; her voice was rich and highly trained. She was the wife of Theodore Gnaedinger, a Montreal furrier, and was going to Paris with their 12 year old daughter Miss Nichol for singing lessons.

That voyage across the Atlantic took 10 days and was the beginning of my 43-year friendship with Mrs Gnaedinger. She was a talented writer and her letters to me, before and after the First World War until she died in 1952, are the most original I have ever received. Although striving after the maximum artistic effect she never repeated herself as my bundle of her letters demonstrates.

My twelve weeks in England were mostly spent visiting my parents, relations and friends. Five weeks at home in Dorchester, where I played the organ at the mid-week services at St Peter's church - a few days in London with friends; at Sammy Woods' magnificent home in Hornsey and Cyril Skinner's in South Kensington - and a few days at Gt Wenham Place where many of family foregathered each year, although the farm was still being run by father's bailiff, Mr Steward. For transport in Suffolk I used my father's pony chaise. In London I had a drive in Mrs Skinner's motor-car, a Landaulet. In Cambridge I visited my sister May and also called on Cyril Skinner who entertained me to breakfast in his rooms in St John's College; a meal I particularly remember for the basket of freshly gathered strawberries and a large jug of cream!

Returning to England on board the S.S. Dominion in May 1909

On a visit to Gainsborough, I called in at Marshalls works and met up with George Borns and Bernard Collett; the latter was leaving for Canada the following week to marry Miss Rose.

Reliving the old days, four of us packed a boat with a tent, rugs and provisions and rowed down the Trent to Addlingfleet where we camped for the night. We were up and breakfasted by 4.00 am the next morning; then we crossed the Humber and rowed with the incoming tide up the Ouse to Goole. After a short break we rowed on up the Derwent to Budwith where I found a telegram waiting for me at the Post Office.

It was an offer of a job for a few weeks with my old firm Clark, Forde and Taylor, to test a cable being made for the Anglo American company; I had contacted them in the hope of getting some work and earning some money. The job was to start immediately and so I left my three pals and made a night-time dash by train via Selby, Gainsborough and Totley to Sheffield where I caught the 4.00 am Scotch Express back to London and went straight to their offices.

The work involved testing German Atlantic stock cable and sheathing in the contractors' works at Enderby's Wharf, Greenwich. Mrs Atkins had offered me a room for the duration at Herne Hill and, by the time I reached there that evening, I was completely exhausted, having only slept for a few hours the previous two nights.

At about that time I received a letter from Paul Schioler of the Winnipeg City Engineer's Office saying that there would be a job for me there when I returned, so I contacted CPR to find out when their next liner was due to depart for Canada. As soon as the final tests on the 100 miles of cable were completed, I cleared up the tackle at Greenwich, went to the office to collect my pay cheque and said goodbye. That evening I left London for Dorchester with my baggage, which included a couple of new suits I had had made in Bond Street (a grey suit for 45/-) and Oxford Street (a blue serge one for 3 guineas).

I spent a week with my parents and my sisters May and Clara in Dorchester and met up with Cyril Day and several other old friends. My cousin Harold Sears came for the weekend; he was then an Engineer Lieutenant and arranged a day out for me on HMS Superb, one of the three new Bellerophon-class dreadnoughts recently commissioned by the Royal Navy to build up their fleet. I cycled to Weymouth and we went out to sea from Portland, but it was too rough for gun-layers' trials.

After a couple of days of final shopping and packing, the family all came to Dorchester station to see me off with my cabin trunk and bag. From Waterloo I went to Mrs Atkins' at Herne Hill for the night and caught the special boat train from Euston early the next morning. Arthur Atkins met me at Liverpool Riverside and saw me onto the SS Empress of Britain, which sailed that evening, August 27th.

Return to Canada - August 1909

The Empress of Britain and its sister ship the Empress of Ireland had been built in Glasgow in 1906 for the Canadian Pacific Railway Co; the first of a fleet of Royal Mail steamships for their Fast Atlantic Service. Three out of the four of us in my 2nd Class cabin spent the first day on our bunks without food to stave off seasickness. On the second day I had 'a light refreshment of jelly and milk pudding' and spent a few hours on deck, but there was a strong wind and the sea remained rough. It took us only 3½ days to sight Labrador, seeing icebergs and displays of the aurora borealis on the way.

R.M.S. EMPRESS OF BRITAIN
14,000 TONS

Before docking at Quebec City, we all had a medical examination and the customs formalities were carried out on board - a great convenience. Several of us disembarked at Quebec and took the train to Montreal where I arrived just 6½ days after leaving London! After two nights in the Welland Hotel catching up with my Montreal pals, I took a train to Winnipeg, arriving on September 7th with only $35 in my pocket and no job to go to. But then began what proved to be some of the most colourful experiences of my life.

Winnipeg, Manitoba – 1909 to 1911

On arrival in Winnipeg I took a room at 158 Smith Street, went for a walk to see the completed Redwood Avenue bridge and had dinner with Alex Gray at Mrs Mac's in York Avenue. The next morning I phoned Paul Schioler and arranged to meet him and Col. Ruttan at the City Engineers' office. He gave me a letter of introduction to Mr Chace of Smith, Kerry and Chace, Consulting Engineers, who offered me a job as an inspector in the field at $75 per month with accommodation in a tented camp. It was equivalent to $110/month in the city and I accepted it with alacrity.

Appointment as Inspector on Transmission Line Construction

Thus, on September 9th, two days after my arrival in Winnipeg, I had a job as a steelwork inspector on the erection of the steel towers for the 77 mile long, 66kV electricity Transmission Line from Winnipeg to the City's hydro-electric plant being built at Pointe du Bois on the Winnipeg River. I had a briefing in the office from Messrs Chace and Kerry and we arranged to meet at the CPR station on Monday. My diary records details of my first days on the new job:

13th September 1909

Raining heavily most of the morning. Leave my lodgings. After lunch meet W.G. Chace (my senior boss) and J.J. Aldred (my immediate boss) the Field Engineer of the new Transmission Line, at CPR station and am told to buy a ticket for Lac du Bonnet. This expenditure of $5.00 left me with a light purse - less than $1.00 - but also with a light heart.

The train crawled away from the city and, after sundry stops, reached Beausejour to give everyone a rest and an opportunity to have a meal in the small township. Jumping into a 2-horse rickety buggy we three, together with a few others, were driven to the King Edward Hotel for a 15-minute supper. Then we were whirled, or rather bumped and jolted, back to the train, the engine of which decided at that moment to do a lot of shunting work.

However, in a little over 4 hours we reached Milner, a deserted lumber camp. Borrowing a hurricane lantern from a man living in a caboose, we found a log shack with shelves for bunks and hay for bedding. An old stove stood in the centre of the shack and scattered around were the ancient and un-attractive-looking clothes of the former occupants, lumbermen. Mr C and Mr A turned in in one bunk, having only one set of blankets, and I lay down on an opposite shelf. I had thought that the place was completely deserted, but I was deceived as I quickly made the acquaintance of the lumbermen's closest companions, fleas. I was soon covered with the marks of their affection for me, for they had not fed for nearly 6 months when the camp was closed down. It took me many days to catch and kill the last of the biters for I had been attacked from my neck to my feet.

14th September 1909

Rising at 6 am we soon had a good fire going. Whilst endeavouring to pour a little water from the kettle into the frying-pan, to par-boil the bacon and remove the salt from it before frying, I emptied the lot onto the fire putting it out! Thus, my first job for the City of Winnipeg was not a success! However, this was soon remedied, and a breakfast of fried salt bacon, pork and beans was quickly demolished. Before leaving we boiled some eggs hard in the unwanted tea and drenched the fire. We left our blankets to be forwarded by the next train and made our way into the bush. The trail was bad and difficult to follow and we were soon wet through to the thighs from yesterday's rain. Besides my camera, I was carrying a pack containing provisions, frying pan, boiling pot, plates (made of birch bark and costing 10 cents a dozen) and cups.

Three miles of the wood trail brought us to the right-of-way of the City's new Transmission Line; a clearing 100ft wide from Pointe du Bois to Winnipeg, a distance of 95 miles. Although all the trees had been felled, they had not been cleared away. For 10 miles we followed the perfectly straight course NE, a tramp the like of which I had never before experienced. For the greater part of the way we walked in a muskeg, sometimes a tamarack swamp and sometimes an open swamp. The stumps of the trees had not been grubbed out and were mostly hidden by masses of moss and other vegetation. This meant 'high-stepping', for one could not tell within 2 feet at what level one's foot would reach bottom. At one step the foot would sink through the moss and go down ankle-deep in water, the next step would be high and dry on a hidden stump. Though the swamp and right-of-way was level it seemed like a continuous up-hill climb. Crawling over fallen, half-hidden timber also slowed our progress. By working hard to keep a good pace we may have done about 2 miles an hour but never more. Where the moss seemed more level, it was like walking on a carpet spread over soup. The water oozed through as a large area of the closely woven vegetation sank under our weight, but without tearing and letting us through. If we jumped up and down on the carpet the small tamarack trees on the edge of the 100 ft right-of-way bobbed to acknowledging our presence,

Seeing a large brown patch without vegetation and rushes, I made for it until I was stopped by a warning cry. It was 'soup' without the cover of a carpet. The only animal life, beside mosquitoes and black-flies, were occasional woodpeckers and a whisker-jack (magpie) which watched us as we quenched our thirst at a water hole close to the log shanty of some men working on the clearing.

The log shanty beside our right-of-way

We looked into the log shanty; it was crude and filthy inside with a sticky mess in a dirty frying-pan on the table and a few empty bottles of Perry-Davis Pain-Killer, which consisted mainly of opium and alcohol.

Water-holes were welcome at intervals and we endeavoured to standardise the flavour at each with the addition of lime-juice. When we stopped for lunch Aldred dug a water-hole with his hands and waited for the muddy sediment to settle until the water became the colour of cold tea, but with quite a different taste. We made a fire and Mr C, by mistake, 'boiled' the tea which we had with fried salt bacon, followed by toast, butter and jam. After a short rest, we set off again and passed one or two small gangs of men grubbing and ditching. Near Lac du Bonnet Mr C sent me on a side trail to fetch a rail hand-car and take it up the CPR tracks and the City's tramway line to meet them where the right-of-way joined the railroad. This done we reached Lac du Bonnet and its 'back-of-beyond' hotel at 7 pm. After a wash, a meal, a walk to the general store with Aldred and the sewing of a couple of bags for sampling cement, I turned in, but not to sleep, because of the companions I had acquired the previous night in the log shack.

Lac du Bonnet

We spent 10 days in Lac du Bonnet before Aldred, Walter McGibbon (my assistant) and I moved out to our first camp at Bear Springs. During that time my job included taking cement samples from the box-cars delivering cement to the site, overseeing the making of sample forms for the flexible tower footings and walking along the right-of-way with Aldred, checking and correcting the setting-out of the tower foundations. We visited the peat fuel factory where a large gang of CPR men were working on the track and checked the gravel samples from the gravel pit 4 miles from Lac du Bonnet, where stripping was taking place in preparation for screening.

These daily trips often involved many miles of walking but whenever possible we used a 'speeder' or hand-car on our construction track. I found that if the load on the speeder was not properly balanced it made the 'pumping' awfully hard and the speeder sometimes left the track. Except for the early morning train, there was no time schedule for the trains delivering steel and other materials to the project. One day I unexpectedly met a train with less than 150 yards in which to get off the line. I lifted the outrigger and wheel and pulled it over me so that I fell, with the whole machine on top of me, into the ditch, just in time to avoid a serious accident, as the train would not have been able to stop in time.

McGibbon travelling by 'speeder' (hand-car or jigger) on the track

There was a CPR branch line from Winnipeg to the terminus at Lac du Bonnet. From Lac du Bonnet to Pointe du Bois, a construction 'tramway' had to be built for the City of Winnipeg to carry men and materials along the route of the Transmission Line and to the site of the new Dam and Powerhouse.

Camp at Bear Springs

The three of us left Lac du Bonnet on the City tramway train, taking our tent, blankets and provisions with us and were dropped off at Bear Springs, a point in the woods about 6 miles from Pointe du Bois. It was a Sunday afternoon and so, after pitching our tent and making up our beds of balsam and spruce brushwood, we took the hand-car and pumped up to Pointe du Bois where we looked over the City Falls on the Winnipeg River and had supper

The route of the Transmission Line from Winnipeg to Pointe du Bois

The distances (in miles) from Winnipeg
to the places along the Transmission Line to
Pointe du Bois were:
Elmwood (6)
Birds Hill (12)
Beausejour and Tyndall (42)
Brokenhead River (49)
Milner Camp (59)
Lac du Bonnet (67)
Bear Springs (89)
MacLarens (92)
Pointe du Bois (95)

at The Residence, which had been built to accommodate the City engineers on the project.

We spent the next few days walking the right-of-way, locating the roads and checking the tower locations. Then we left the hand-car and tent, stopped the City train and went back to Lac du Bonnet and on by CPR to Beausejour where we put up at the King Edward Hotel for the night. From there Aldred and I inspected 30 miles of the Transmission Line route to Birds Hill, travelling in rigs with a pair of horses and driver. On Saturday, when we had finished at Birds Hill, we walked to Elmwood and took a tramcar from there into the centre of Winnipeg where I spent the weekend with my pals, Pearson and Gray.

After a visit to the office to collect the mail on Monday morning, Aldred and I returned to Birds Hill Station and walked to the No.1 Camp of the Williamson Construction Company, 5 miles from the station. Williamson had the contract for the construction of the Transmission Line and for providing camp accommodation along the line for the City's inspecting engineers.

The camp of tents - mine was 7ft x 9ft with a 4ft wall - was pitched on top of a hill covered with a black sand or earth; black dust pervaded everything, including food and clothes, and made us all and our possessions filthy. Furthermore 'the eatables were very poor and the meat indescribably tough'. Bread and pastry were dark brown when the wind blew whilst the cook was mixing and baking them and this, together with the rancid and 'green' butter, made the meals distinctly unappetising.

We were there for a few days during which I made my first visits of inspection to the gang of 18 men erecting one of the steel towers. They were using 2 pneumatic riveting guns driven by a portable gasoline engine compressor. One hand riveting gang on the flexible tower were doing a very poor job and the looseness of the strap bracing members gave me a lot of trouble. I also inspected the work of the concreting gang as well as the unloading of steel at the Birds Hill Sand Company's siding.

Camp near Birds Hill

On October 9th I packed up my dunnage and took down my tent for the move to No.2 Camp, 3 miles east of Birds Hill about 12 miles from Winnipeg. E.H. Cotterell was leaving for Winnipeg for the weekend and I slept in his tent until mine was ready – the asbestos ring for the stove not having turned up. I also took over his concrete inspection duties in addition to keeping an eye on my steel gang. At least the cook in this camp was better and we had an excellent supper of canned salmon, potatoes, prunes and pie.

My home from October 1909 until November 1910

My visitors from Winnipeg – Pearson & Gray inside my 7ft x 9ft tent

The next two Sundays I walked into Winnipeg, the 12 miles to Louise Bridge taking me 3 hours. There I met up with Gray and Pearson and some other friends; we had chats, a walk and a meal at 263 York Avenue before I returned to the camp. The walk back in the dark was rather frightening as the howling of the coyotes seemed quite close at hand. One Sunday I walked a total of 29 miles, including a 5-mile walk with the boys in the afternoon. For a change occasionally, Pearson and Gray would come out to the camp for a weekend, have dinner and spend a night in the tent with me.

My diary records an amusing incident at that camp: 'Capt. Graham fired 3 revolver shots at a spruce grouse (rather larger than a partridge) sitting on a rock about 2 ft square. He hit the rock but did not disturb the bird, which looked round at him and us. Billie Campbell (time-keeper) came up and, at about 20 paces, fired 5 more shots, all of which came near to the bird. It was still undisturbed by three more shots from Cotterell, who, advancing on his belly, fired lying down at about the same distance. The bird then gave a chuckle and flew away before Jack Brown, the owner of the gun could fire. Seven shots had hit the rock at the bird's feet.'

The spruce grouse, sometimes called the 'fool-hen', relied on its camouflage and on remaining motionless for its protection. Once I shot four of them off a tree, carefully potting at the lowest one first so that, in falling, it would not disturb the others! They attracted attention to themselves by calling when they saw a man, but they were good eating, except for a slight flavour of spruce buds on which they fed, and they provided a welcome change from the eternal hot sow-belly or beef stew in the construction camp.

The arrival of winter brought relief from the myriads of flies in the cook and dining tent. By the end of October the temperature had fallen to zero Fahrenheit at night and there were magnificent displays of the aurora borealis. The temperature fell further to 13 degrees below zero (45 degrees of frost) in November and it was not easy to get water. The melting of snow in a bucket on my wood-burning stove gave me soft water for my laundry and for bathing in the tub, one leg at a time, but I had to refill a bucket with snow several times to get a bucketful of water, for 10 inches of dry snow melted to produce only 1 inch of water.

My tent furniture consisted of a sheet iron stove, a camp-bed, stool, table, bench, bucket and dipper and basin. There was no chair and of course no bath in the camps, so I, like all the men, had to have a wash all over in a small tub of water. When camping close to a river we could get water more easily without melting snow. The method was to dig a large hole in the ice with an axe as deep as the axe-handle would allow. Then, by firing a rifle bullet through the rest of the ice, water would well up and fill the excavation which was big enough to immerse the bucket. At night and during the day the hole was covered up with an empty box and some canvas to keep it from freezing up again.

The camp staff consisted only of a cook, 'cookee' and 'bull-cook'. The cookee prepared the vegetables and washed up after the meals; the bull-cook kept the cook supplied with wood for his cooking stove and fuel for all the sheet iron stoves in the winter.

One bull-cook, whom I remember as popular with everyone was young Bronco, an ex-Barnardo's boy. It was generally accepted in those days that about 98% of all boys and girls selected for emigration from Dr Barnardo's Homes in England made good and became useful citizens, many becoming prosperous. Bronco used to come to my tent for a chat and I feel that I may have helped him in building his character.

I acted as the camp doctor but had only three medicines: capsicum (extract of red peppers used to treat diarrhoea and stomach ailments), laudanum (a tincture of opium used for pain relief and cough suppression) and cascara (a laxative). Bouts of dysentery or diarrhoea were not uncommon in a camp of men having no sanitary arrangements.

As work extended further from the camp, the daily tramp along the pathless Transmission Line reached up to 18 miles a day. Because of the labour and expense of moving camp, it was delayed until we had to walk 9 miles each way to and from work, taking up too many daylight hours. Moving camp in winter was a big job and involved the work of all hands, work on the Transmission Line being stopped during the process. The walls of the tents became thick with ice, for, as the snow which fell on the roofs melted, the water froze on the walls making them thicker with each snowfall and all the more difficult to move.

Back to civilization briefly

In early November, the camp moved nearer to Winnipeg, within 2 miles of the CPR crossing, and so visits there became easier and more frequent and civilised meals were obtainable. I was able to walk to and from the city and the camp and still continue my daily inspection of the towers being erected along the line. Sometimes I called in at the office and went with A.S. Vowell to inspect the steel in the Manitoba Bridge and Iron Works before it was delivered to the site. Vowell was a graduate of University College London and had been involved in the steel design for the new

Victoria Station in 1900 when the terminus of the London, Chatham & Dover Railway was merged with that of the London, Brighton & South Coast Railway.

I had rented a room at 133 Smith Street for a month and 'felt like a Sybarite, sleeping between clean sheets instead of rough blankets'! During those 4 weeks in the city I met up with Pearson, Gray, Evans and Tabernacle in the evenings, frequented our usual cafés, played the piano at sing-songs at 263 York Avenue and went to church on Sundays.

One Sunday Pearson and I went for tea to the Deanery at St John's Cathedral with the Rev. and Mrs Coombes where we met their daughter Marjorie (who 'came out' this year) and Miss Holmes. It was the beginning of my friendship with Marjorie and she and I had a long talk before we all went to the service in the Cathedral. Pearson and I met up with the girls again the following evening at the Arts Exhibition at the Royal Alexandra Hotel, the CPR hotel which was then the social hub of the city.

In mid-December I returned to the camp when it moved to Riva's Swamp, a very sheltered spot with spruce trees forming splendid protection from the wind. However, I went back to Winnipeg for a few days over Christmas. Pearson came to my room on Christmas Eve and 'we ate almonds, raisins and cherries and read some ballads from 'Songs of a Sourdough' about life in the Klondike Gold Rush by Robert W. Service', whose poetry had become a favourite of mine.

On Christmas Day we walked to Deer Lodge and had a splendid ten course lunch ($1) washed down with a pint of claret (75c.), followed in the evening by an excellent supper at Mrs Mac's with music and songs; we ended up at the Royal Alexandra Hotel listening to the band and watching the 'swagger parties' there.

I had breakfast at Mrs Mac's on Boxing Day and spent the morning there reading and playing the piano. That afternoon

Pearson joined me to go to the Coombes' for tea, talk and music; Marjorie and I played the piano (Peer Gynt Sunset and some Beethoven) and everyone sang songs: Nazareth, My Ain Folk, Old Folks at Home and Toll for the Brave! Pearson and I left at 11.30 pm and had 'a little supper' of buckwheat cakes and maple syrup at the Olympia on the way home.

The Rev. Dean and Mrs Coombes, Marjorie, and Bernie at the Deanery

Deer Lodge, Winnipeg – Christmas 1909

Main Street, Winnipeg

A 'pile of water'
after a fire in winter

Winter of 1909/1910 – Camp at Brokenhead River

I left Winnipeg after Christmas with E.A. Bartlett (who was from Weymouth) and A.D. Smith and we spent a night in the King Edward Hotel, Beausejour, 28 miles NE of Winnipeg. My cheeks froze two or three times the next morning as we were driven 7 miles by sleigh against a bitterly cold north wind to the camp at Brokenhead River.

The winter was undoubtedly colder than usual for northern Manitoba and the temperature in the early mornings when I got up was 37 degrees below zero. Although it rose to 5 below zero by noon, the wind chill from the accompanying gale made it feel far colder. I stayed a night in Bartlett's tent before my own, ¼ mile away at the steel camp, was put up. We chatted and he talked chiefly of his prowess as a rifle shot, an engineer, a hunter, etc... The moonlight was so bright that one could almost read by its light inside the tent at night. I spent the following days inspecting the erection of the towers, which progressed despite the exceptionally low temperatures and strong wind. A steel gang of 11 men plus a foreman normally completed the assembly and riveting of one 'braced' and one 'flexible' tower a day. When lack of coal for heating the rivets in the forges stopped the riveting for a day or two, I went on to inspect the pile driving operation. With two gangs working I regularly inspected over 730 rivets driven in a day.

The first six days of January were exceptionally cold and the lowest temperature, on the 4th, must have been 52 degrees below zero (84 degrees of frost) for the spirit in my thermometer left the lowest graduation (-47 deg.) and shrunk into the bulb! The men worked on the steel towers all day but watched each other very closely for signs of frozen noses or cheeks. Ears were always covered and felt boots or moose-skin moccasins were large enough to accommodate several pairs of socks – I sometimes wore seven pairs! Even in February the temperature fell to 45 degrees below zero on at least two nights.

The 20th January was a brilliantly fine day with a wonderfully clear atmosphere, and we had an excellent first view, just after sunset, of what we thought was Halley's Comet. It was in the lower western sky with its long tail above it. Over the next week it appeared larger and brighter as it moved higher and away from the setting sun. We learnt afterwards that it was not Halley's Comet, which was due 4 months later, but one unexpected by astronomers which became known as the Great Daylight Comet of 1910 as it was much brighter than Halley's and could be seen in daylight. Halley's Comet arrived on schedule in May and was visible by the naked eye at night for a week or two; I got up at 3.45am on a couple of night to see it.

During the days when I was out on my inspections, the bull-cook would arrive at the job at noon with a 'dixie' of stew for the gang and would build a fire to thaw out the frozen meal. We all sat around the fire, piling a thick blanket of dry snow over our feet and legs to prevent the moccasins or felt boots from becoming wet as a result of the fire's heat on our snow-coated footwear, for both moccasins and felt boots soaked up moisture like a sponge. I had ordered a new pair of moccasins from an Indian woman; she looked at my feet and said they were as long as her forearm, and of course she charged me accordingly.

When not visiting or being visited by Bartlett or others, I spent the evenings in my tent writing my reports and letters to my friends and family; also reading and studying some engineering books which I had borrowed from the library in Beausejour. We were driven there occasionally in the single rig to go to the post office or do some shopping and generally had a meal at the hotel before returning.

Sundays were a good time to do my laundry in the soft water of melted snow, to sew on any buttons, repair my trousers or mend socks and tidy the tent. I had sewn up my blankets into a sack so that I had several thicknesses above and below me. I then inserted my rabbit-skin blanket into the middle of this 14-thickness sleeping bag and could slip into any higher layer when the weather was warmer. Bartlett came to cut my hair, using a newspaper as a sheet with a hole for my head. Occasionally he and I would go out with guns and come back with a brace of partridge for supper. One Sunday, Vowell and I went for a 3 mile walk on the ice down the Brokenhead River and saw several tracks of mink and 'fisher-cat' (the fisher is a small mammal of the weasel family, slightly larger than a marten, which is trapped for its valuable brownish-black fur) – he wanted to see where to set his traps.

I had had the good fortune to buy my rabbit-skin blanket from an Ojibway Indian; it was made from perhaps 100 thick white, winter-killed rabbits. The skins, each cut spirally into a long, half-inch wide strip, became ropes of fur for the strips curled to form a tube. Apparently these ropes of fur were woven on a 6ft square frame, with nails to hold the ends which were secured by a strip of woollen material before removal from the frame. Thus there was thick white fur on both sides as well as filling the holes. I have never seen another like it, except in a Canadian film in which an Indian Chief was shown wearing one as a regal cape. With my covering of grey flannelette to prevent the fur eventually coming away, this blanket lasted me for years and was used later as my sleeping bag in France during the First World War.

At minus 30 degrees (62 degrees of frost) my alarm clock would stop; presumably because the oil froze. At such a low temperature, and when the fire in the stove had gone out, I shivered and ached in every bone in spite of my blankets and rabbit-skin robe. The night watchman, who kept the fires going through the night, seeing no steam or smoke from my tent-chimney, would come across and re-light the fire. When the stove dampers were sealed at night there was enough leakage of air to convert the green wood into charcoal. On opening the dampers first thing in the morning, the charcoal would burn furiously, and the stove became red hot so that the temperature in the tent could rise to 100 degrees! The tars also condensed on the inside of the chimney during the night and sometimes caught fire so that the chimney emitted showers of sparks from the burning tar. In spite of the tent being made more or less fireproof by alum, small holes would be burnt by these sparks.

A temperature of zero Fahrenheit in my tent was the highest I aimed for at night as that was comfortable in my blankets. The bucket of melted snow standing on the ground inside the tent would be solid ice in the morning. By placing it in the top of the red-hot stove I got a bucket of hot water in a matter of minutes. It was then no hardship to get out of bed, open the flaps of the tent and perform my ablutions. As the temperature in the tent rose it melted the frozen ground under the floor boards and brought to life a large frog which, with his croaking, thought that spring had come. It must have seemed a very short summer when the camp moved and he froze up again.

On one cloudless morning in February, with the thermometer at -35 deg. (having risen from minus 45 deg. at sunrise), I saw and sketched the sun at 9.15 am with its four sun-dogs, a further concentration of light above the sun, and 22 degrees further up an inverted rainbow - a circumzenithal arc - with its legs sticking up into the sky. I saw the same effect in January a year later from noon to 3 pm. The sun-dogs, sometimes called parhelions or mock suns, and the circumzenithal arc were both caused by the refraction of light through hexagonal ice-crystals in the upper atmosphere.

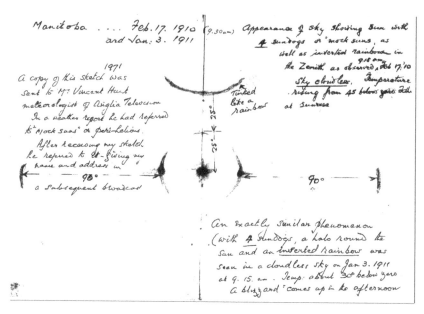

Manitoba .... Feb. 17. 1910
and Jan. 3. 1911

(9.30am) Appearance of sky showing Sun with *4 sundogs* or mock suns, as well as inverted rainbow in the Zenith as observed, Feb 17, '10

9.15 am
Sky cloudless. Temperature rising from 45 below zero at Sunrise

Tinted like a rainbow

1971
A copy of this sketch was sent to Mr Vincent Hunt meteorologist of Anglia Television. In a weather report he had referred to "Mock suns" or peri-helions. After receiving my sketch he referred to it - giving my name and address in a subsequent broadcast

25°
25°

90°   90°

An exactly similar phenomenon (with *4 sundogs*, a halo round the Sun and an *inverted rainbow* was seen in a cloudless sky on Jan 3. 1911 at 9. 15. am. Temp. about 30° below zero. A blizzard comes up in the afternoon

My sketch of the sun-dogs and the circumzenithal arc above

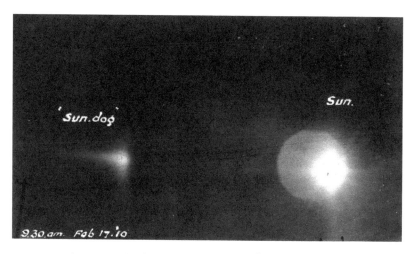

Photograph of the sun-dog on 17th February 1910

From a minimum temperature of -36 degrees at the end of February, only a month later in March, I recorded the remarkably high temperature of 72 degrees in the shade – a rise of 108 degrees

Fahrenheit! On that day I ran back ¼ mile to the riveting gang, stopped their air-compressor set and made the men fight a fire which threatened the forest. I had no idea whether we could extinguish the flames, but succeed we did, saving hundreds of acres, perhaps many square miles, of jack pines dry as tinder on an equally dry forest floor, for the winter's snow had sublimated (evaporated) rather than melted. Smoke from forest fires sometimes darkened the sky for days and one was never quite sure whether they were miles away in the US, in Wisconsin, Washington or Idaho, or whether they were closer at hand, which would have been frightening.

There were many camps at intervals along the line of towers and I regularly walked miles between them on my inspections, looking for damaged steel, loose bracing and poor riveting. It was 10 miles from my camp at Brokenhead River to Milner camp where I normally met up with Chace or Aldred. Sometimes we would go on to Holmes camp and stay a night or two at the Lac du Bonnet Hotel to witness the unloading of car loads of steel and concrete caps for the tower footings.

The Lac du Bonnet Hotel

The Lac du Bonnet Hotel described itself as 'the last hotel between civilisation and the North Pole'. It was built entirely of wood with a shingle roof and the walls between bedrooms were nothing more than half inch tongue-and-groove boarding; so thin that you were disturbed by anyone snoring in an adjoining room during the night. The fire escape was simple; a rope, long enough to reach the ground, was fastened in each bedroom to the windowsill. All you had to do was open the window and slide down the rope.

Just outside the main building was a 'bunk-house' where hoboes and drunks were sent. I remember one night an unholy noise came from downstairs when a half-breed with money in his pocket demanded a bedroom, not a bed in the bunk-house. The fat landlord tried to throw him out but was impeded by his pyjama trousers slipping down from his very convex stomach. One of my assistants, a hefty young Englishman, ejected the man without difficulty and silence returned to the hotel.

We all fed in the one dining room. Besides the landlord's wife, there were two other women – a waitress in the dining room and a chambermaid. The rest of the staff consisted of a barman and the old handyman who kept the furnace going and did odd jobs. He used to go round the upper floor waking everyone with his rich voice intoning 'Its 6 am and a beautiful morning to boot! The breakfast is ready, and the girl is waiting to wait. The CPR train leaves in an hour, the City train in two or three hours 'perhaps'! Time and tide wait for no man, nor does the CPR.' He had evidently been in an English choir many years before and his morning 'muezzin' will never be forgotten.

It was not unusual for a lumberman arriving at this, the first hotel he came to after finishing his winter's work in a lumber camp, to hand the landlord $200 to board and feed and keep him supplied with all the whisky he wanted until it was all spent. The first few drinks which he got were probably good liquor, but once under the influence he was given anything that would keep him fuddled and happy. When the money had almost been spent, the landlord very wisely handed him back his last $10 to ensure that he could pay his fare on the train and leave the district.

The Camp moves closer to Pointe du Bois

At the beginning of March the camp moved to a location 2 miles west of Lee River, not far from the Winnipeg River camp and 7½ miles from Lac du Bonnet. From there I was able to spend only the occasional weekend in Winnipeg and go to the theatre or to a concert with the boys. These visits were brief and infrequent so that my social engagements and contacts with feminine society during that time were very few.

One such occasion was on Easter Sunday, when I went to the Deanery with Cecil Pearson and Percy Tabernacle for tea with the

68

Dean, Mrs Coombes and Marjorie, who had just returned from the season in Ottawa. After attending the service at St John's Cathedral we had supper and some hymns before leaving. On another occasion the four of us played some bridge. That trip to Winnipeg also enabled me to get some serious dental work done, two roots pulled, my plate fixed, and an abscess lanced that had been giving me terrible toothache.

St John's Cathedral, Winnipeg, close to the Deanery

In my reply to an offer from my old firm, the Canadian Inspection Company of Montreal, to take over from Innes as their district manager in Winnipeg, I said that I would not accept less than $135.00 per month, a figure I did not expect to be agreed. To a later and different offer I asked for $160.00 and, by showing it to Mr Chace, I got an increase in my own pay to $100.00 per month with everything found.

The next camp was only 4 miles from Beausejour. It was the end of April and signs of spring were everywhere as butterflies emerged and green shoots appeared on the vegetation. However, the warmer weather brought out the mosquitoes and flies which were in evidence indoors and became particularly troublesome in the swamps. Flocks of wild geese flew north to their breeding grounds in perfect v-formations and the whip-poor-will (like a nightjar) started singing its monotonous song punctually at 8.45 each night. It was mating time; the drumming of a cock partridge on a stone to attract a mate sounded like the motor of a launch starting up in the distance and the white-throated sparrow sang its 'Oh-poor-Can-a-da' song from which it was given the name, the Oh Poor Canada bird.

Being close to Beausejour gave me an opportunity to borrow and read some rather different books, instead of my usual selection on science, philosophy, and religion. Perhaps as a reaction to the very 'male' life of the camp and my recent acquaintance with Marjorie Coombes, I took to reading some romantic novels such as Madame Albanesi's 'Little Brown Mouse' and H.G. Wells' novel 'Love and Mr Lewisham'.

The death of King Edward VII was reported on 6th May and correspondence from our SKC office began arriving in deep black-bordered 'City' envelopes; the ones from the Manitoba Iron Works were decorated in black and purple. Although his death marked the official end of the Edwardian era, the social legacy of the pleasure-loving, cosmopolitan monarch lasted until the outbreak of War in 1914.

Camp life – Summer and Winter 1910

The Williamson Construction Company was providing our inspectors' camps at a cost of $50 per week, plus 50 cents/night for keeping the stove fires alight. Camp life was tough and crude; far, far cruder than would be tolerated today. The men, some of them little more than hoboes, together with me and other visiting engineers and inspectors, had all their meals in the cook-tent at plain board tables with forms for seats. We were each given a knife, fork and one spoon. No spoons were pro-vided for service from dishes so that after helping oneself to soup, one would lick the spoon clean and help oneself to the everlasting meat stew, and then later to the stewed fruit or pie. One's hobo neighbour did the same.

I saw that the cook, on getting out of bed in the morning, would slip the pan of bread dough between his blankets so their warmth would cause the dough to rise. Blankets were never washed! A cleaner way would have been to put the pan on the top of a barrel in which a hurricane lamp was alight and holes had been drilled for air to reach the lamp.

In summer the flies, together with the unattractive hot and always greasy food, brought me down below par. Temperatures of 99.2 degrees in June were over 150 degrees warmer than a few months before and in mid-July the temperature inside my tent at 4.00 pm reached 110 degrees. Camp life without cold food, salads and fresh fruit became almost unendurable; far worse than the below-zero weather. House flies swarmed over the food in the cook-tent and at night they settled in black masses on the underside of the tent roof. Couple this with the fact that there were no proper latrines and it is a wonder that there was so little disease in the camps. However, I did develop stomach trouble in mid-June and had to spend a week in Winnipeg on sick leave to recuperate.

Away from the cook-tent with its swarms of house flies, other flies pestered us throughout the 24 hours. Black flies that cut holes in one's face or committed suicide in one's eyes, sand flies which were almost invisible but caused extremely painful stings and the ubiquitous mosquitoes, all working in three 8-hour shifts! To avoid the mosquitoes when eating our lunch we sometimes climbed the newly erected towers and sat on a cross arm many feet up where there was a slight breeze and no mosquitoes.

The Transmission Line Camp Crew

The steel erection gang

The engine and air compressor for the riveting gang

The construction and erection of the Transmission Line towers

Our Construction Railway and the City Train

As Lac du Bonnet was the terminus of the CPR branch line, we had to build a 28 mile extension tramway for the City of Winnipeg through the boreal forest and over the Winnipeg and Lee Rivers to deliver steel, cement, machinery and construction staff to the Transmission Line and to the Dam and Powerhouse being built at Pointe du Bois.

The tramway was crude compared with standard railway practice. Much of the track was laid on muskeg, a mattress of more or less decayed vegetation, without any solid foundation. We had not attempted to remove the mattress and fill the voids below with unlimited ballast, but instead relied on the mattress to carry the train. So, to spread the load on a greater width than that of the sleepers, trees were laid between the sleepers making a 'corduroy' bearing surface perhaps 25 to 30 feet wide. Fishplates joining the rails could only have their bolts tightened at one end for the long trucks caused the track to heave up between the bogies, sometimes touching the underside of the freight-cars!

The City of Winnipeg's only locomotive on our track
across the muskeg

74

Our one and only passenger car on the City train was heated in winter by an iron stove with a loosely fitting chimney protruding through the roof. On one occasion, after steel for the towers along the line had been unloaded we found that snowdrifts prevented the engine from moving the train, except by retreating some yards and then charging at it, pushing it a few feet each time. It was a painful experience standing in the passenger car, watching the approaching headlight of the engine, waiting for the bump and holding on to the hot stove and chimney to prevent them from collapsing onto the wooden floor.

On another occasion, having noticed that the flanges on the front wheels of the passenger car had worn badly, so that there was nothing to prevent the derailment of the front bogey, I decided to get off the train and walk behind it when we came to a trestle bridge!

Unloading steel from the freight train near the camp

Crossing the Winnipeg River on the new bridge

Corduroy road construction over swamps

Tree trunks used to form a 'corduroy' base for a
road or rail-track over muskeg

Oxen delivering tree trunks for the corduroy road

We used horses to move materials to where they were needed

A pair of horses harnessed ready to pull a double horse rig.

Arthur Mitchell

Our train, with its ancient passenger car at one end, discarded by some USA railroad, and the rest consisting of CPR freight cars, was run by the redoubtable Arthur Mitchell. Once, when the train and we, the passengers, were waiting for him, I saw him coming from the hotel in no fit condition to act as conductor-guard. So I ran to the engine and told the driver to get going! Arthur made a desperate run and we could see his dismay, but fortunately could not hear his language, on seeing 'his' train leave without him. McGibbon was with me and I asked him to collect the fares in place of Arthur.

Not long before, Arthur had carried out an unusual task. Two undesirable women from Winnipeg, not allowed accommodation within the limits of the construction camp or township, installed themselves in a disused log shanty alongside the track and away from the camp. He ordered them out and, setting fire to the log shanty, ensured their departure from the district.

Arthur Mitchell was a well-known local character and a few years before had been a mail carrier, by dog team in winter and canoe in summer and by God-knows-what method between seasons, through slush and along the half-frozen river, between Lac du Bonnet and the survey parties working towards the hydro-electric scheme at Pointe du Bois, some 30 miles away as the crow flies.

Then, when the City's construction railway had been built, Arthur became the train conductor cum assistant manager. He had 'married' an Indian girl of the Ojibway tribe and they had a family of 4 children. His cheerful personality made him extremely good company when he was sober but better avoided when drunk. If he could have written his autobiography, it would surely have become a best-seller.

I could write of many of his exploits and escapades for I came into contact with him almost weekly during the building of that part of the Transmission Line which paralleled his railroad, for we were dependent on his train for transport of ourselves and materials. He was, I believe, killed whilst serving with the Canadian expeditionary force in France during the First World War.

Birds Hill, Elmwood and Mud Lake Camps

In June and July our camp moved, first to Birds Hill and then to Elmwood, close to Winnipeg, where I spent the occasional evening and weekend with the boys. There I was occasionally entertained by the Rev. Coombes and his family, or by my chief W.G. Chace, in their homes, where my music after dinner proved a great asset. I played at services at the little church by the new Powerhouse site and when a lecture was given there by Bishop Lofthouse of Keewatin on his great journey to the Arctic.

In June the Dean and Mrs Coombes celebrated their Silver Wedding with a garden party for 350 people at the Deanery. I sent them a silver mounted bridge set ($6.50) as a present but was unable to attend the party, not being prepared with a top hat and dress suit which was 'de rigeur'. Pearson went to the party and became a regular visitor to the Deanery, staying there sometimes with his sister in the absence of the Dean and Marjorie.

On July 14th the St Andrews Dam (on which I had worked for six months in 1909) and Lock was formally opened by the Prime Minister, Sir Wilfred Laurier, with the Minister of Public Works, the Hon. William Pugsley. Laurier was one of the great Canadian statesmen; he had been PM since 1896 having won four consecutive elections. He was the first Francophone prime minister and his policy of moderation and reconciliation had been instrumental in bringing together the English and French into a Canadian nation.

Two days later, on my 28th birthday, my diary says that 'I made all sorts of resolutions regarding conduct, etc.'; unfortunately I cannot recall any of them and did not write them down! The boys took me to dinner at Mrs Mac's in York Avenue and on the Sunday I was invited to tea at the Deanery. After the service at the Cathedral the Dean and I attempted Schubert's Symphony in B minor before we joined the ladies in the garden. 'We had gramophone selections and then supper. I left at 10 pm with a candle wrapped up in a 3ft roll of newspaper by the Dean for my tent'!

The S.S. Winnitoba at the St Andrew's Dam, Winnipeg

As a birthday treat to myself I arranged a trip with Arthur Booth on the recently built S.S. Winnitoba to the see the completed St Andrew's Dam. There we were shown over the Dam and Lock by Innes, who had been appointed Lockmaster.

In August the gangs started putting up the Transmission Line towers using shear legs to raise them to the vertical position onto the foundation caps. Chace asked me to calculate the sag curves and work out sag sheets for the lines and inspect the cable stringing. I had a good chat in the office with him and, at my suggestion, he agreed to make me responsible for all the work on the towers, including the cable stringing and painting of the transmission towers, and he promised to process my salary rise quickly.

In my spare time I had been browsing through gun catalogues to try to decide what gun would be most suitable for me. C.A. Clendenning offered me some advice and came with me to Hingston Smith Arms Co.'s gun shop in the city to look at a few rifles. My choice was between a .303 British Winchester US Carbine @ $31 and a .303 Savage @ $26.50. I chose the Savage, which together with a case, rod and cleaning kit, cost me $32.75. We then went to Eaton's, then known as Canada's Greatest Store, where I bought a Williams shot gun for $37.50. Eaton's had opened 'the big store' in Winnipeg in 1905 as the centre for their catalogue and mail order business which was flourishing in the West.

At the beginning of September the camp moved to Mud Lake, near the new Pointe du Bois Powerhouse at the 'beginning of the line'. The Residence at Pointe du Bois was a very comfortable and commodious log-built club-house which had been built for the bachelor members of the City's staff of engineers on the project. I often stayed there, sharing Harry Wilson's room with J.M. Leaney, and joining in social evenings with the engineers, staff and some of their ladies. We played a lot of bridge and I was very much in demand for piano solos, songs and as accompanist for violin solos. One evening after supper 'Miss Grace Gunn and Miss Cairns came in and we had music: Roy Gunning singing, Cameron and Stamford on violin and self and Miss Cairns on the piano.' Sometimes I was invited to the homes of the married engineers for an evening of supper, music and bridge. After dinner and the usual gramophone selections, we took two canoes out on the river one evening and raced each other, paddling around the big island above the falls before sunset.

One weekend I walked with my rodman, G. Sproule, to Rice Lake Camp, both of us carrying our double-barrelled shot-guns. Leaney joined us and we took a canoe out onto the lake and paddled into the centre of a large wild rice field, but we shot nothing. We had more luck on other outings and on Thanksgiving Day at the end of October the sky became black with wild duck on their evening flight; I shot two mallard and secured one of them before we had to paddle hard back to shore through quickly forming ice.

A propos wild rice, I saw in a press cutting in November 1969 that: *To persuade rich Americans to spend more money and impress their guests, wild rice is advertised as the correct accompaniment to wild duck. It costs anything between £2 and £3 today!* Wild rice, with its long black grains, was formerly eaten only by North American Indians. We watched the Ojibways harvest it on Rice Lake by beating the tops of the reed-like plants into their birch bark canoes as they paddled through the self-sown field. Walking back from the lake in the dark past an encampment of their tents, we saw the Indian boys treading out the rice by the light of their lanterns.

Whilst our camp was so close to Pointe du Bois I stayed at the Residence whenever I could and had hardly slept in my tent at Mud Lake before it was moved to MacLarens, the next camp, at the end of September.

MacLarens Camp

My second winter in camp was spent in a larger tent, 12ft square with a 6ft high wall, which I was allocated when we moved to MacLarens. The camp was situated beside the construction railway track and I used the train as my means of sending mail and reports to Winnipeg.

A train ran two or three times a week passing our camp at 5.45 am on its way to Lac du Bonnet. I would emerge from my sleeping bag at about 5.15 so that when the driver sounded the whistle ½ mile away I had time to put on some clothes, buckle on my felt ankle slippers and, with a hurricane lantern, go and stand on the track waving it to signal the driver to stop. This he would do, so that the last car, the only passenger one, was close to me. I would then board the car, hand my letters to Arthur Mitchell with instructions to buy stamps or postal orders, and then climb down the steps and wave the lantern for the driver to proceed. With the outside temperature sometimes down to 30 degrees below zero it must have surprised the passengers inside the car to see a lightly dressed man emerge from the woods for a chat with the conductor. But in the very dry winter air it took more than ten minutes to get really chilled so long as there was no wind. It was easier, when warm from the blankets, to put on trousers than it was in the daytime when fingers were too cold to do up the buttons – zips were not invented then.

In the following weeks I travelled between the camp and Lac du Bonnet, Tyndall, Beausejour, Birds Hill and Winnipeg, visiting the rock drilling, riveting and steel erection gangs on their various jobs, climbing the towers to inspect the insulators and paintwork and reporting to Aldred and Chase. These trips involved many miles of walking between the camps and the towers and, if I was working near the camp, I sometimes took my shot-gun with me. During one walk back to camp I shot 8 partridges, a hawk and a rabbit, the partridges being no sport as they refused to fly. Five of the partridges I sent to Mrs Coombes and received a very appreciative letter back.

On the longer trips near the construction track I used the speeder when I could, but for travelling from Lac du Bonnet to Winnipeg we used the CPR train; it was a 'mixed' freight and passenger service. Once, after I had been a few days in the bush, I boarded it to go to Lac du Bonnet and on entering the only passenger car, I was greatly embarrassed to see several Winnipeg City officials and engineers, as I was unshaven, dirty and generally scruffy. So, as the train slowed up at the terminus, I leapt from it, ran across to the hotel, shaved, changed my collar, tie and jacket and completely changed my appearance before meeting the officials when they arrived at the hotel!

That was not the first time that I had jumped down from a train moving quite fast. I once had a useful lift on our railway on a special train carrying British MPs and other VIPs in Pullman cars to see the hydro-electric plant under construction. It was hauled by a heavy CPR locomotive as well as our engine, and so was able to climb gradients which were steeper than normal for main lines. The train was travelling slowly up such a gradient as it approached my tented camp, 6 miles from its destination. Not wanting to have to walk back to camp, I jumped and fell sprawling on the ground, having underestimated the speed of the train and the height of the Pullman car step from the ground. I got up and walked as if this was quite normal until the train disappeared from sight, then, and only then, did I feel myself over for bruises and any damage!

Years later in London, travelling every morning on the Underground in the days before car doors were only opened automatically when the train stopped, I used to choose the front coach so that on approaching Mansion House station, I could leap out and be propelled by my momentum up the stairs at the station.

My larger 12ft x 12ft tent at MacLarens Camp

For my own interest and in order to record progress of the work as it progressed, I took many photos, including some of the men, and I became the unofficial camp photographer. I regularly sent rolls of film to R. Strain & Co in Winnipeg for developing and printing, once sending as many as 18 films and receiving 170 prints! There was quite a demand for my prints, and I made a few dollars selling copies to Chace, Vowell and the others as well as including them in my reports and, of course, in my own album.

Before the real winter set in, a weasel became almost tame running around my tent, sniffing at the stocks of both rifle and gun which may have been used during the day. Their movements are exceedingly quick so that rarely is one fast enough with a gun to shoot them – they seem to move just as the trigger is pulled! But they are easily trapped and that, to my sorrow and disgust, was the fate of mine, caught by the camp cook who did a little trapping of fur animals in his spare time. Although it was beginning to turn white it was too early in the winter for the fur to become ermine and even an ermine skin was worth only 25 cents.

Hunting Big Game – December 1910

Below-zero weather started suddenly with -18 degrees at the end of November and intensified during my 5-day big game hunting trip in early December. The Manitoba big game season lasted only from December 1st to the 15th.

Mackay, D.J. Black and I set off on our hunting trip on 3rd December. We followed a trail made by a dog team and set up camp in a primitive shooting lodge at Shell River. We took with us as a guide called 'Butcher', an old Indian, who with his dog team brought a large load of blankets and provisions for us from Pointe du Bois. By the time we returned on the 7th we had shot one bull moose and two caribou, the limit allowed by law; one animal for each of the three of us, not counting the guide.

A carriole, with unusual decorations.

A dog team and cariole (a dog-drawn toboggan) with its decorations

On the first day out we went west and north of the camp following fresh trails, zig-zagging across them until we discovered they were of a cow moose. We then traipsed through muskeg following other trails with no success. 'It felt like walking in a country filled with sponges and fallen trees - the whole levelled off with soft deceiving snow.'

We followed the Winnipeg River on the second day, walking 20 feet apart with Butcher leading and frequently testing the thickness of the ice with his axe. After 1½ miles we turned west and had lunch in a tamarac swamp. In the afternoon we came across fresh tracks and stalked these over the ridges. Peering into the next valley we saw three large black forms; all three of us shot at the largest, a bull moose, which we dropped. Butcher cut up our moose, leaving the head, skin and quarters in the woods for the dog team to recover the next day.

After a breakfast of moose steak (without salt) the next morning we walked ½ mile up river and then turned north. We had lunch on a ridge and that afternoon came across some fresh caribou tracks in the valley which increased in number as we followed them. On seeing the caribou we watched them for a while and then fired; the startled bunch ran towards us and then scattered. I got shots at two, one of which was a fine buck which Mackay finally dropped, and someone dropped the other. By then it was late afternoon and, having only disembowelled them, we left through difficult bush for camp. The next morning Black and Mackay went with Butcher to skin the caribou and I walked the 10 miles back to Pointe du Bois. My account of this trip was published in 'Rod and Gun' magazine in January 1914.

An incident at MacLarens camp a month later, when I broke the Canadian game laws in three places, has to be recorded. It happened when I returned to the cook-tent to have my midday meal instead of roughing it with the men. There I found Arthur Mitchell, who had come prospecting for suitable trees for the thousands of cords of firewood required at the new hydro-works some 6 miles away. I had seen some fresh moose tracks close to the camp and invited Arthur to my tent to tell him so. He had no rifle so he suggested that we should both follow the trail.

A certain way of telling whether a moose was close by is to plunge one's bare hand deep into a footprint to feel if the snow, forced up between the toes of the cloven hoof, had had time to become a knife-edge of ice. If not, the animal had passed within minutes; it was also possible to identify the direction in which the moose had been travelling.

Soon we came to where the animal had lain down and it had, as usual, urinated on rising. This gave evidence, quite obvious to Arthur, but not noticed by me at the time, that we were following a cow moose. He was careful not to tell me for he felt that I might call off the hunt and he wanted the meat. Very soon we sighted the animal and I exclaimed "Oh, it's a cow!" Arthur, simulating great surprise, said "Why, so it is!" I am afraid that he rightly guessed that I would yield to temptation. After I had dropped it and before we set to work to skin and gut it, jobs which were impossible once it had frozen solid, I took a snapshot of it and then stupidly left my camera hanging on a nearby tree, giving all the evidence required for my conviction on three charges of breaking the game laws:

-   shooting a cow (never allowed);
-   in January, over a month after the end of the short hunting season; and
-   having no game licence.

Before leaving the carcass (and my camera on the tree), we used our snow-shoes to cover it with a couple of feet of soft snow, partly to hide it but also to prevent it from being frozen to the ground before Arthur could come and remove it. He was, of course, delighted when I said that he could have it for it was doubtless worth $25 to him and he came with his dog team the next day to collect it. His squaw would make good use of every part of the moose – the skin for moccasins, the sinews for sewing them, the meat for food, the fat rendered down for lard and the offal shared with the huskies. I retained the moose's head which I had stuffed and mounted by a taxidermist in Winnipeg (for $15) before shipping it back to England, to my parents' home at Wenham Place.

The bull moose we shot

When I got back to camp to leave my rifle and go back to work, the camp cook met me and asked if I had shot anything; he had heard two shots! I remembered that the Government offered $25 reward leading to the conviction of anyone breaking the game laws. When he asked for some of the meat, for he said that he was getting short of beef for the men, I wondered if he wanted it as proof of my quilt. I told him that I had given the carcase to Arthur Mitchell but later we did have moose-stew. The cook, good fellow, did not let me down.

The moose's head dominating the hall of my home in England, with the splendid head of a jumping deer which I shot in 1911

JANUARY, 1914   FIFTEEN CENTS

ROD AND GUN
IN · CANADA

AFTER MOOSE AND CARIBOU
IN MANITOBA

H. C. Lott

THE district near the mouth of the White Shell River where it empties into the Winnipeg River was, in 1910, the scene of a successful hunt with rifle and camera. The Manitoba big game season lasts only from Decemer 1st to the 15th and therefore the number of filled licenses depends largely on the weather conditions during those two weeks of "still hunting."

On December 3rd, David, George and I set off from the nearest point on the railroad to locate our camp, which was to be a partly completed log shack, eleven miles away, which was being built for a survey party by the well-known Indian guide, Butcher and two "breeds."

The trail, made by his dog-team a few days before, was easy to follow in the dense bush, but when it emerged on to the ice of the river, it was invisible, the wind-driven snow having obliterated all traces. Had the ice been strong enough the whole trip would have been down the Winnpeg River with only a few diversions to short clean-cut portage trails at the falls. But the quiet bays were the only safe weight-bearing parts of the river, where we found the trail, by feeling with our moccasined feet for the frozen ridge under the snow.

Reaching our destination at 3.30 p.m. we found Butcher with his two helpers packing the chinks of the half finished shack with moss. Though he had almost completed a day's work and had made a few short journeys for wood with his dogs, he readily agreed to drive them to our starting point and bring back our blankets and provisions that same evening. This twenty-two mile trip through the bush, the trails strewn with fallen trees, was very different to the usual run on the river ice, and must have sorely tried the old fellow, who was over sixty years old. While waiting for him we sat under the sloping Indian shelter in front of a great campfire, by the strong light of which one of the photographs shown was taken.

Soon after midnight the dogs, drawing the neatly loaded sleigh, arrived, followed in a few minutes by their master uttering maledictions upon their heads for having bolted from him when he had stumbled in the dark. A hot supper and a few drops from the "medicine bottle"

90

Winter of 1910/11

We had had a splendid banquet at the Residence in mid-November to say farewell to A.D. Harris who was leaving for another project. The evening concluded with a long toast list and musical programme after a great feast which included: oysters, olives, oxtail, salmon, sweetbreads, turkey, pie, ices, dessert, punch, champagne and port. I played a piano solo and accompanied others and replied to the toasts of 'the Transmission Line' and also 'College Days' as there were several English college graduates present.

As the winter advanced and my tent walls became thicker with ice, I imagined that it would have stood up without poles. The ice did at least reduce the effect of the cold wind outside, although there was not much room in the tent and I had to sleep quite close to the walls, which remained frozen even when the stove was red hot. When there was a blizzard, I found it difficult to keep both sides of myself warm and would turn into my sleeping bag early in the evening.

In the virgin forest, the footprints of the wild inhabitants of the bush appeared all around the tent after each fall of snow. The snow prints included deep holes left by moose, caribou and jumping deer and patterns left by timber wolf, coyote, fox, lynx, otter, mink, marten, snow-shoe rabbit and muskrat, down to the tiny field mice in their travels from one grass stem above the snow to the seeds at the top of the next one. In less than a week a very close and intricate pattern revealed the presence of a large population which the human intruder rarely ever saw, for most of the animals moved about at night. Even the spruce grouse dived into the snow to spend the arctic night, emerging in the morning leaving a tunnel with droppings inside to show the night's lodging of this stupid bird.

And then a fresh fall of snow would settle and the surface printing started all over again. Only the woodsman could read their stories from their tracks; the tragedies and the struggles for life of the denizens of the forest.

During the winter months the contractor's gangs had one or two accidents whilst erecting the towers: tower FM13 was damaged as the shear legs broke when it fell during lifting – unlucky 13, and it was a Friday too! Two other towers buckled when the shear legs slipped off their footings. Fortunately, these problems were not too difficult to resolve and no one was hurt.

In addition to the erection gangs we had Swedish and other European workers, in pairs, who had been given small contracts for ditching and clearing on the right-of-way for the line. Their tastes were basic as I learned when doing a few shopping commissions for them. For instance, when asked to buy some butter, I was told that it didn't matter if it was a bit green or rancid. I don't remember margarine being available in those days. In the extremely hot summers, with temperatures in the 90s in the shade, it was not surprising that food changed its appearance and flavour!

Before and after Christmas I spent a few days in the Winnipeg office where Chace asked me to measure the drainage area of the Winnipeg River (52,000 sq. miles) and its tributary the English River and to calculate the flow duration curve, as well as to estimate the total length and weight of the Transmission Line cable. Fortunately, these tedious office jobs were interspersed with some regular steelwork inspections.

Making the most of a short stay in the city, Pearson and I went skating on the Assiniboine River ice-rink and, after a dinner at the Angelus Café (35c.) one evening, I went with D.A. Evans to a performance of 'The Chocolate Soldier', a new operetta (1908) by Oscar Straus based on Bernard Shaw's novel 'Arms and the Man'. 'It was a fine piece and a great improvement on the musical comedy of the day.' Mr and Mrs Chace were most hospitable and treated me to dinner one Sunday before we went on to the Band

Concert at the Walker Theatre - they also invited me to join their New Year's Eve party with Bill Stamford, Dr and Mrs Dory, Miss Leach (from Toronto) and Miss Bessie McGillivray; 'we had music and bridge until midnight and Bill and I walked home at 2 am'.

I went back to The Residence in Pointe du Bois for Christmas Day and played the organ at a well-attended service in the Schoolroom conducted by Rev. Allison. Christmas dinner at 4 pm that afternoon was 'an elaborate and enjoyable affair with several courses, wines and music.' The Ladies entertained us on Boxing Day to a Christmas Tree from which we were each given a silly present, mine being a miniature violin, others receiving such things as a baby's feeding bottle, teething ring or doll, after which 'the whole party, including the contractor's staff, became juvenile and frolics and noise ruled until two sets of Lancers were danced and we all went to bed'!

During January and February I spent most of my time with the gangs erecting the towers along the line, walking between them and the camps. Sometimes I stopped over for a night at Lee River or in Leaney's tent at Bouthilliers Camp and I also spent a few nights in Winnipeg whilst inspecting the Red River Towers. Whilst there Chace held a Valentine's Bridge Party for 8 of us including the Fergusons, Miss McGillivray and Miss Cornell who played the piano with me.

From Winnipeg I went back to the camp where I had my meals, but I took a room at the Lac du Bonnet Hotel and spent most nights there in March; it was much more comfortable and not far from my inspection work on the Winnipeg River Tower, the High Tower and Disconnecting Switch Tower.

Looking back (in 1966) on my 7 years spent in Canada, I realise that I enjoyed fewer strokes of the exceptional luck than came to me in later years. However, one occurred on March 11th, during the in-between season when the thaw was beginning, and ice was becoming unreliable.

I had just inspected the work being done by two men at the top of the 100ft tower built on a rock in the Winnipeg River. The rock was separated from the mainland by a narrow channel and, in crossing the ice on my way back, I broke though it into the fast-flowing water up to my hips. Throwing myself forward on to the unbroken edge of ice which fortunately bore my weight, I was able to get out. Upon reaching land, I shouted to the men that I was going back to Lac due Bonnet to change my clothes. They had not seen the accident so I could have disappeared under the ice without their knowing it.

Crossing the river by our 1,000ft long wooden railway bridge I encountered the 4-man track maintenance gang who offered me a lift on their hand-car. But that, in the near zero Fahrenheit weather, would probably have meant frozen feet and legs so I walked the rest of the 2¼ miles to the little back-of-beyond hotel at Lac du Bonnet, not without some difficulty because my trousers and overalls had combined to freeze into pipes, giving me very little room to bend my knees. After changing into dry clothes, there was of course no bathroom in the hotel, I went back to the job across the bridge.

100ft Tower on a rock in the Winnipeg River

The City of Winnipeg's railway bridge near Lac du Bonnet connecting the CPR terminal at Lac du Bonnet to the hydro-electric plant at Pointe du Bois

1911 - Spring at the Pointe du Bois Powerhouse and Dam

In mid-April, on instructions from Chace, I left my work on the Transmission Line and reported to W.M. Scott to join his staff supervising the work on the Powerhouse at Pointe du Bois. This move caused me come anxiety - I was not sure what the future held and my plans for going to England for a holiday seemed to be knocked on the head.

My first job, with which I was totally unfamiliar, was to estimate the quantities of cement required for the Powerhouse. It involved spending the next few weeks of April and May in the draughting room on the boring task of calculating concrete quantities from drawings. Meanwhile Chace had decided it was necessary to strengthen the retaining walls of the canal and forebay and to build a crest of 1:4:7 concrete on top of the dam.

Office hours were 7 am to 4 pm with an hour for lunch. After work I would go for a walk before supper with one of the other engineers, Rupert Howard, Bill Stamford or J.F.I. Thomas of Vickers & Maxim, to the end of the rock-fill dam which was progressing across the river. Although there was still nearly 100 ft of the river to be closed by the rock-fill, the upstream level was rising, and water was starting to spill over the spillways.

Just before the Easter weekend a blizzard blew down two of the flexible towers which should have been more securely anchored until they were grouted. This accident came as somewhat of a blow to my fairly successful reputation on the Transmission Line construction. It was also a serious set-back for Chace and the firm's reputation, as public opinion had already lost faith in this type of flexible tower after several accidents had already occurred whilst the towers were under construction.

Fortunately, the incident did not overshadow the party which Chace had arranged at the Powerhouse for the Easter weekend. He and Mrs Chace arrived on the train from Lac du Bonnet with G.Y. Smallwood, Miss Bessie McGillivray and Miss Rowena Bourne, both sisters of engineers on the project. Everyone stayed at The Residence for the weekend and we had bridge parties and dinners followed by music and singing, Miss Bourne having an excellent trained soprano voice. I think the Rev. Allison must have directed his sermon that Sunday at me, saying, 'for if Christ is not risen then is my preaching in vain!' I had recently declared to him my unwilling disbelief in the Christian faith.

Life at The Residence was a wonderful contrast to tent life in the camps. As the weather warmed up in May, Jack McGillivray and I spent a weekend fixing up a tennis lawn which became well used in the evenings and we also made good use of the Hunting & Fishing Club at Trout Lake. Bill Stamford, with his wife and young son and Butcher, the Indian, came back from one outing having landed 36 fish weighing 90 lbs into their canoe from four trolling lines. There was also sailing on the lake in the big canoe with its 75 sq.ft sail and, on 4th June, we had our first dip in the water. It all seemed too good to be true – and it was! Chace told me at the end of May that I was to take over from Aldred as Field Engineer for the Transmission Line and so my stay in The

Residence came to an end, except for the occasional weekend visit during the summer.

Since one of my jobs was to produce an estimate of the total cost of the project I kept a record of the payroll costs of our project team:

Transmission Line Staff during the Location of Towers – June 1909

J.J. Aldred	Engineer	$ 150 per month
A.S. Vowell	Steel Inspector	$ 100 + board
A.D. Smith	Telegraph Inspector	$ 100 +
J.B. Bourne	Transitman	$ 80 +
W.S. McGibbon	Rodman	$ 50 +
Taunton	Concrete Inspector	$ 75 +
Corble	Cook	$ 60 +
Harper	Axeman	$ 35 +
Sinclair	Axeman	$ 35 +
Parkhurst	Axeman	$ 35 +

Additional Transmission Line Staff – April 1911

H.C. Lott	Steel Inspector	$ 100 + board
J.R. Watts	Cable Inspector	$ 100
J. Riddell	Steel Inspector	$ 70 +
W. Todd	Telegraph lineman	$ 50 +
J. Kolinsky	Axeman	$ 2 per day

Engineering Field Staff Payroll at Pointe du Bois - 1911

W.M Scott	Field Engineer	$ 250 per month
O.B. Bourne	Assistant Engineer	$ 115 + board
J. McGillivray	Assistant Engineer	$ 100 +
W.L Stamford	Instrument man	$ 100 +

C.V. Cameron	Draughtsman	$ 60 +
Geo. Meighan	Rodman	$ 50 +
Geo. Sproule	Rodman	$ 50 +
J.F. Cullen	Rodman	$ 50 +
E.E. Maulson	Rodman	$ 50 +
W.D. Mulkian	Structural Steel Inspector	$ 120 +
J.M. Leaney	Electrical Inspector	$ 75 +
W.S. McGibbon	Clerk	$ 70 +
Jas. Smeaton	Snr Construction Inspector	$ 120 +
J.F. Gillbanks	Snr Construction Inspector	$ 120 +
E.B. Patterson	Jnr Construction Inspector	$ 75 +
John Mackie	Jnr Construction Inspector	$ 95 +
W.J. Brogan	Cook	$ 55
Mrs Brogan	Housekeeper	$ 30
Paul Dowell	Cookee	$35
Mrs Butcher	Laundress	$ 35

West end of Power House temporary board wall removed.

May 12/11.

The Pointe du Bois Powerhouse under construction – May 1911

The Pointe du Bois Hydro-electric Scheme completed

Field Engineer on the Transmission Line

When I left The Residence at Pointe du Bois I went back to the Lac du Bonnet Hotel initially and from there I began a detailed examination of the progress on all the towers on the line. The months of June, July and August were hot and humid with occasional heavy thunderstorms. The mosquitoes were extraordinarily active and maddening, driving us crazy during our daily inspection visits and making 'out-of-doors' impossible in the evenings. 'Had a miserably uncomfortable night with the heat and mosquitoes' on 16th June; 'some must have got through the screen on the window'. I even watched a moose as it lay down in a swamp to get rid of the pesky insects, raising its head and flapping its ears!

During weekends at the hotel I was reading a recently published book called 'The Nature of Man' by Ilya Metchnikoff, the Ukrainian zoologist who won the Nobel Prize for Medicine for his discovery of phagocytes (macrophages) and their role in the human immune system. He was strongly influenced by Darwin's work and did not believe in the immortality of the soul. He was also credited with coining the term gerontology for the study of aging and longevity. It was most interesting and, for me, a relaxing contrast to my long days along the line to inspect the work, my basic technical and social discussions with other engineers and writing up my notes and reports in the evening.

I also took the opportunity whilst living by the Lac to learn to swim – something surprisingly I had never done before. McGibbon came with me to begin with and gave me some instruction so that, after much practice I was able to swim 25 yards by early August, having started learning in June.

During those three summer months I visited all the towers and the camps at Brokenhead River, Milner, Lee River, Beausejour, Molson, Tyndall Booth, MacLarens, Birds Hill, and Schmidts. On these trips I sometimes stayed a night at the Beausejour Hotel or the Red Deer Hotel at Tyndall, and, on visits to the office in Winnipeg, I took a room at the Empire Hotel or Corona Hotel.

As well as keeping an eye on the erection of the towers, my inspections also included checking the ditching and corduroy road making, the construction of a patrol house and the sinking of a well for fresh water at Tyndall Booth, which, even after being bored through limestone to 110 ft. had still not hit potable water.

As my inspection of the contractors' work along the line involved tramps of up to 24 miles a day, I hired the speeder or took a double horse rig whenever I could. When the ground was very soft in summer the horses sometimes floundered in the mud; then we would have to unhitch them, pull the buggy out and re-harness the team.

In June, Arthur Mitchell's wife developed smallpox and he and his family were moved to an island and quarantined. People in Lac du Bonnet and Pointe du Bois were also quarantined as a few cases developed in both places, but not before we had a celebration at Pointe du Bois to mark the Coronation of King George V on 22nd June.

On 1st July McGibbon and I were vaccinated by Dr Goulden on his visit to Tyndall before he went on to vaccinate the residents of Lac du Bonnet and Pointe du Bois. Fortunately, the outbreak did not spread and after three weeks the quarantine was lifted.

Our Winnipeg office was now located in the Carnegie Library Building and I worked there with Clendenning to complete an estimate of the final cost of Williamson's Construction contract for the Transmission Line, including the Patrol Road and all the other extras we had agreed. This took me almost a month, often working from 8 am until late at night.

The Winnipeg Annual Exhibition was in full swing and it was Citizens' Day on 19th July when I had my first sight of an aeroplane in flight; it was a Wright biplane piloted by Coffyn who flew a demonstration circuit for about 7 - 10 minutes.

Coffyn flying a Wright Bros biplane at the Winnipeg Exhibition

Canoe trip on the Winnipeg River

In mid-August, during a 4-day break from my inspection work, 'Mac' McGibbon and I made a canoe trip down the Winnipeg River from Lac du Bonnet to Fort Alexander, which was then only a Hudson Bay Company post on the Lake at the mouth of the river. With no settlements, not even two houses together, between Lac du Bonnet and Lake Winnipeg, this trip was full of adventure, hardship and some discomfort, making it the more delightful to recall.

For the trip we borrowed a very old 18ft canoe, which we soon discovered was heavier than we expected from its many coats of pitch and paint, and also a tent which proved to be very far from rainproof.

Starting with a favourable breeze, we sailed across the Lac du Bonnet, calling at various landing places and shacks to locate Arthur Mitchell, for we needed him to act as our guide and to help in carrying the canoe and dunnage over the portage trails.

Arthur had, by then, lost his important job as assistant manager and general factotum of our railroad having once gone berserk when he and his Ojibway 'wife' and children had been quarantined during the smallpox epidemic on an island in the river. Becoming restive for lack of action and liquor he had hi-jacked the boat taking supplies to the island, gone ashore, got drunk and gone into the station office and smashed up the furniture. For this he was fired. In spite of his faults, Arthur was an excellent canoe-man, hunter and woodsman and extremely good company.

Mac and I eventually ran Arthur to ground at 'Boucher's Point'. Looking particularly scruffy and unshaven, he explained that he had just come back from hunting moose; it was of course out of the official season, but he had shot a young moose from which he gave us some steaks. He asked for time to shave and to change his trousers, for both legs were showing through, so Mac and I made temporary camp and had a meal. Arthur introduced us to

Boucher, a French Canadian, and suggested that he should join us; he would be useful with the heavy canoe and was a good cook of flapjacks and cookies!

Boucher's contribution to our provisions was a bucket full of caviar, perhaps 5lbs or so, from a large sturgeon which he had just landed and which he had salted for keeping.

Our canoe was loaded almost to the gunwales as we sailed back across the lake with four men plus dunnage, tent, shotgun and food, We encountered heavy waters and on more than one occasion I left the decision as to whether we should venture from the shore to Arthur, saying that his life was worth more than ours for he had a wife and 4 kids. As an expert canoe-man, he always squatted in the stern and steered, all four of us paddling against the stretches of whitecaps, for the fresh winds made progress slow and sometimes quite hazardous.

At the Upper and Lower MacArthur Falls where we had our first portages, and the ¾ mile portage past Big Bonnet Falls, we found that our canoe, emptied of course of all its contents, was so heavy that it had to be carried on the shoulders of two men. These were the first of 9 portages on the journey to Fort Alexander. Two of the others – at Bear Falls and Bouthillier's Falls - were sometimes avoided by shooting the rapids when going downstream. However, with our canoe heavily loaded, we did not attempt those, so that eighteen times on the relatively short double journey we had to unload the canoe, carry it and all our dunnage, reload and launch at the other end. By using tumplines, two of us managed all the loads, the other two humping the canoe on their shoulders.

The longest 'carry' was past the Big Bonnet Falls, a drop of 35 to 37 feet, where the ¾ mile portage felt much longer than its name. Since those days the rapids between Lac du Bonnet and Lake Winnipeg have been flooded out by dams and hydro-electric schemes which have been built at Pine Falls (1952) and McArthur Falls (1954).

Canoe trip on the Winnipeg River

Temporary camp with Mac McGibbon, Boucher and Arthur Mitchell

The rapids on the Winnipeg River near the MacArthur Falls

We certainly needed a guide like Arthur, who knew the river, to show us where to land at the head of the several falls and rapids and the route of the narrow portage trails which, with the lush undergrowth, were not always easy to follow in the bush. In some cases the portage was over rocks, without any indication of direction for the remainder of the trail.

It was near the foot of the Big Bonnet portage that we found an 18ft canoe, left by a Government survey party. It was nearly new and very much lighter than ours. It had been left in the shade and was full of water to prevent shrinkage and thus keep it watertight. So we wisely, if illegally, made an exchange for the remainder of our journey to Lake Winnipeg, trusting that the new canoe would not be required during our short absence.

When we had passed the Lower Bonnet Falls where we made a 600 yard portage over rock, we decided to camp for the night. After supper of moose steak, Mac and I put up our tent which proved to give little protection from the thunderstorm which soon soaked our blankets from above but also underneath, for we had failed on the sloping ground to cut a trench around the back of the tent. It was a very disturbed night for me and I had to wake Mac to help me dig outlet ditches inside the tent to get the rush of water away. Then, giving up, we spent the rest of the night in our sodden blankets.

At daybreak, we built a fire to dry ourselves and our clothes. We had a breakfast of caviar, bacon and marmalade, watching a fresh rain shower till 9.30 before we loaded the canoe again and started downstream.

In the first few hours of a canoe trip, the novice with legs doubled up under him for the correct squatting position, has to beg the other paddlers to stop whilst he straightens out one leg at a time to restore circulation. We never knelt or sat, but always squatted like the Indians for both safety and the more effective use of the flat-bladed paddle.

Again the wind was against us, making very rough water through which Arthur steered us safely, all four of us paddling. At Silver Falls there were two short but rather dangerous portages where we had to take the canoe very close indeed to the top of the falls at both landings. However, there was an alternative ½ mile long carry which we took on our return journey. In the afternoon the water was less rough and we made better progress to our destination at Fort Alexander, but everything was soaked afresh in another rain storm.

Reaching the Fort at 6.30 pm, we headed straight for the only habitation - the Hudson Bay Company's post - and asked 'the Swede' there for accommodation for the night. He was a Scandinavian half breed and the factor at the post. He refused our request saying, 'We do not entertain strangers' to which I replied, 'We do not want to be entertained but will pay for anything we receive'. I pointed out that our blankets were soaked, our tent leaked, and more rain was on its way. Relenting a little, he said that we could help ourselves to wood from the log-pile. Then he suggested that there was a shack a little distance upstream where the young missionary would probably give us shelter for the night.

So Mac and I paddled up-stream in the darkness and were most hospitably received by Mr Eley, the young English missionary, a theological student from Toronto University. He was spending the vacation gaining practical experience amongst the local Indians. Meanwhile our two companions, Arthur and Boucher, had left us to walk to the nearby Indian Reservation to spend the night there and, perchance, to determine whether the reputed aphrodisiac property of caviar, of which much had been eaten during the day, had any foundation in fact!

An Indian family on the Reservation

Eley made up a good fire in his iron stove so that our blankets, hanging from ropes strung across the room, lost some of their wetness during the night. He lent Mac and me a dry blanket and with it we slept well on the wooden floor of the empty room.

The next morning, Arthur and Boucher turned up breakfastless and, to our dismay, we found that husky dogs (never fed in summertime and therefore foraging around for food) had turned our canoe over and had eaten most of our provisions. Eley then generously gave us breakfast and I somehow felt that we had eaten some of the last of his food supplies, a can of pork and beans. Before leaving, I offered to pay for all his help and hospitality, but he refused to take more than a small donation for the Mission. He gave me the impression of finding life in this lonely spot rather frightening, especially as he had found footprints of a possibly drunken Indian who had walked round his shack at night. He had recently been issued with vaccine to vaccinate the local Indians against smallpox of which there were still some cases in the area.

After breakfast, we heated some pitch (or was it balsam gum?) and also used some soap for sealing the cracks in the leaky canoe bottom before paddling back to the Hudson Bay store where we bought some more food for the return journey. Then, in fair weather and with a strong wind, we sailed up-river homewards, making good progress without paddling, for the wind which had been against us was now in our favour.

At Pine Falls we found traces of a sawmill with the remains of a waterwheel at the base of a narrow power canal cut through the rock. Surely this was the first attempt to harness the enormous potential power in the Winnipeg River which now produces many hundreds of thousands of horsepower in the great hydro-electric stations between its source and the Lake. The first major scheme was that at Seven Sisters Falls developed by the Winnipeg Tramway Company. The second was the City's own plant at Pointe du Bois of which we were supervising the construction.

A mile and a half up-stream we came to Bear Falls, one of two that we decided not to shoot; the portage was on an island in the middle of the river. Then another mile further on were the Bouthillier Falls before we sailed 5½ miles on to Silver Falls, arriving there at noon. We landed and unpacked our blankets to give them a final dry-out in the breeze whilst we had our lunch.

We returned the borrowed canoe at the Big Bonnet portage and then humped our heavy old canoe over the mile long carry to the head of the falls where we camped. At supper, Boucher cooked some excellent hotcakes and I had a dip in the pool above the falls before turning in for a comfortable night in dry blankets.

After portaging around MacArthur Falls we attempted to paddle up some rather steep rapids where we were temporarily swept onto a rock, fortunately without serious damage. We said goodbye to Boucher, our older guide, at Boucher's Point and arrived back at Lac du Bonnet that afternoon, sailing and paddling up to the City's railway bridge across the river and hauling our canoe up to the track. After carrying most of our stuff back to Lac du Bonnet, we paid and said goodbye to Arthur Mitchell. With money to burn in his pocket, he was not likely to be very good company that evening.

The next morning, 24th August, I caught the 9 am City train to Pointe du Bois and arrived at noon to start on the final calculation of concrete quantities for the Powerhouse. After 19 months of a nomadic life, spent mostly in tented camps, I enjoyed another spell in proper accommodation at Pointe du Bois and in Winnipeg. For the next two or three weeks I was based in the office at Pointe du Bois completing the concrete calculations. After finishing work at 4 pm, I was able to play tennis at the Residence and go swimming and sailing in a canoe on the lake. As McGibbon was unable to leave his work on the Transmission Line, Frank Cullen became my companion for sailing and canoeing trips in the evenings and at weekends.

One weekend we took the canoe up-river with provisions but no tent and had a magnificent sail, almost to Lamprey Falls. We stopped at a lovely little island and prepared to camp there for the night until we made the mistake of shooting a skunk and so quickly evacuated and moved our quarters to the mainland! We spent Sunday sailing around the lake, shot a duck for the larder and also, to our shame, a porcupine, before ending up near Lamprey Falls for a picnic supper with the Gunns. We sailed to the big island to camp that night in the shack of last year's lumber crew, but it was so unsavoury that we slept outside under the stars until a heavy storm drove us back inside.

Portage

Silver Falls

Our canoe with the sail up on Lac du Bonnet

Prince Albert, Saskatchewan – September to December 1911

During one of my visits to Winnipeg in mid-September to discuss the progress of the Transmission Line with Chace, he said he wanted me to leave that evening for a week or two in Prince Albert, known as 'the Gateway to the North', 750 miles west of Winnipeg. With only my city clothes in my baggage I left on a GTP train arriving in Prince Albert the following afternoon. It was early days in Saskatchewan, the Province had only been formed six years earlier in 1905, and the Grand Trunk Pacific Railway (GTP) had built the first line from Winnipeg to Prince Albert in 1907.

My job was to witness some test boring in the bed of the North Saskatchewan River to find a good foundation for a dam to serve a new hydro-electric scheme for the City. The 'week or two' turned out to be almost 3 months and the temperatures fell 'way below zero' before I got my winter kit and show-shoes.

The morning after my arrival, I called on the Mayor of Prince Albert, Andrew Holmes, and the City Engineer, F.A. Creighton. Their Consulting Engineer for the project, Mr (later Brig.) C.H.

Mitchell of Toronto, had reported favourably on a site some 25 miles from the town. The City Council decided to get a second opinion before raising the capital to finance the scheme and my firm, SKC, had been asked to examine the site and report on the plans of the Toronto engineers. We had asked for more borings in the river to find a suitable location for the dam and I was assigned to watch the work and report on the results.

The Mayor drove me 25 miles in a 2-horse rig along the river road to Steep Creek Post Office, where I was to be lodged with the Cozens family during my stay in the area. On the way, he handed me his gun with which I shot a few prairie chickens and he then used it to shoot some wild duck on the numerous sloughs or small lakes which we passed.

The Cozens, a dear old English couple with a grown-up adopted daughter, were to look after me and I was almost embarrassed by their kindness. Mr and Mrs Cozens had emigrated to Canada in 1883, the year I was born, and must have travelled hundreds of miles in a wagon containing all their belongings to one of the Government's free 160-acre plots. Before marriage, Mrs Cozens had been an assistant cook in an English household employing 30 servants. Mr Cozens had been the junior gardener. She was a wonderful cook, her only fault being to overload my plate for each meal with, for example, a whole mallard duck or two smaller teal.

They lived in house No.2, a long log building, and I was installed in house No.3, not long completed. This was also built of well-chinked logs which were hidden by planking covering the outside. It was a 2-storey building and I was the first to live in it. My bedroom was upstairs, and all my meals were served downstairs in a room which contained an early phonograph with cylindrical records and an American organ!

Having no children, they had driven to Prince Albert to adopt a one-year old girl. She was 21 when I was there and, since that drive 20 years earlier, neither she nor her foster mother had seen two houses together, only single homesteads in the 160-acre plots. The 'girl' was now a hefty grown woman, helping with the farm work and, an excellent shot with rifle and shot-gun, she helped to provide game for the table.

House No 3 of the Cozens' homestead
My home near the Saskatchewan River Sheep Creek Sa

Mr Cozens cultivated only 40 of his 160 acres on which he grew oats every year. He was still harvesting some 50 bushels an acre, so fertile was the virgin soil. Where the land was uncultivated it was used for grazing; wild strawberries flourished there, mushing up the cartwheels of the farm wagon. During the mosquito season, the Cozens lit smudge fires for their cattle which were sensible enough to line up in the plume of smoke as they fed, gaining some protection from the pesky insects.

It was obvious from the costly construction of house No.3 that Mr Cozens' farming efforts had brought him prosperity. When the freeze-up came, he would kill the fatted heifer or bullock which provided them with joints of meat until the break-up of the frost months later. In the summer, they lived on salted meat or game, the latter being in profusion.

The Cozens family with the 2-horse rig

My job, watching the 2-inch cores brought up by the drillers from the river bed, involved a daily trudge of 6 or 7 miles to and from the test-boring plant. It was pleasant enough in the glorious fall weather, but was tiring when the snow came, especially after a sunny day followed by a night frost, when a crust formed on the snow. It would have been much easier with my snowshoes which Gerald Mossman eventually sent from Winnipeg. In those circumstances it was said that a man on snowshoes could run down a moose, which would eventually get exhausted breaking through the surface into deep snow.

The snows came in October and the rabbits' coats turned white, but the earlier snowfalls melted before a white carpet formed over the landscape. It was extremely funny to see white rabbits sitting motionless and dotting the area where none had been visible before! Their habit of sitting still when a man approached had, for the rest of the year, been their protection against predators, for their brown colour blended perfectly with the landscape. However, natural selection, which had obviously favoured those who turned white in winter, let them down at this time of year.

To obtain cores from the riverbed the drillers had a large scow (80ft by 28ft) on which was mounted a steam boiler, engine and drilling gear. To moor in the middle of the river we had to get a heavy rope across; no easy task given the strong current. Just as we had failed, after two days of attempts, a stern-wheeler hove into sight and the skipper shouted that if we had a rope across the river he would have cut it, for it was a navigable river. Fortunately, it was the Government Survey ship 'La Fleur' with Mr L.R. Voligny in charge and, as no other boat would require passage for a few months, he gave us 1,000 feet of Hudson Bay tracking cord which solved our problem. At the same time he offered me a lift to Prince Albert and gave me much useful information about the river during the journey. In return, I helped the 8-man crew winch the boat through the La Colle rapids, assisting the efforts of the 30 HP kerosene engine.

Drilling rig in mid-stream on the North Saskatchewan River

The scow in mid-river with steam boiler, engine and drilling rig

Hauling the boiler on to the middle of the river
Nov: 21. 1911.

Hauling the boiler back to the middle of the river on
the ice – Nov 1911

116

The Government Survey ship La Fleur

I stayed two nights at the Windsor Hotel in Prince Albert and then, as the guest of Mr Creighton, he drove me and the Mayor, Alderman Baker, 'in an auto of Mr Howard Hudson' to Steep Creek. We stopped on the way to do a little shooting, but there the engine failed so Creighton and I had to walk the rest of the way. During the next three days we both watched the drilling and also visited the nearby gold-washing plant of the Saskatchewan Mining & Development Co. That small exploration company promised that if the dam was built they would supply all the sand and gravel, after washing it free from gold.

Even at 44 ft depth the borehole cores were still showing a water-bearing layer of sand and gravel. This meant that we had to move to an alternative site further downstream to try to find a firm foundation and resulted in my staying on until mid-December.

Mitchell's firm of Toronto engineers had been responsible for the Niagara Falls scheme and they recommended an Ambursen dam for this project; it was a 'hollow' concrete slab and buttress design requiring less concrete. The test boring to find a good rock or clay bottom for the dam was being carried out by two skilled drillers with the help of some locals. The drilling team consisted of an American foreman, a Canadian, a Czech and a Russian, a fine

28-year old hard-working immigrant. A young French-Canadian was the dirty, careless and very poor cook, providing meals for the two drillers in a crude log shack which leaked in snowy weather, for there was only straw on the log roof. So with me, an Englishman, we were a cosmopolitan gang of 6 different nationalities.

I had my midday meal in the shack from a perpetual rabbit and partridge stew which the young cook kept supplied with his .22 rifle. He notched up about 40 partridges and a score of rabbits in 6 weeks and must have been a good shot to achieve this with his small-bore rifle. Our hot drink was usually a mixture of coffee and tea for he often did not remove the remains of the last brew. 'If it's coffee, bring me tea. If it's tea, bring me coffee' was our cry from the heart!

Moving the scow took a few days and required the help of four Galicians when it grounded on rocks on its way downstream. The first test-holes in the new site were encouraging but later we encountered water-bearing strata which I determined would endanger the stability of any dam that was built there.

Towards the end of October I gave my report on the drilling results to Adam Grela to take to Creighton in the city; 'Grela is a decent Russian who is working on the gang and takes his oxen to Prince Albert tomorrow; he is about my age and has an outstanding personality and physique'.

I had to go into Prince Albert myself at the beginning of November to see Creighton and pick up some electric exploders which were due to arrive from Winnipeg. I borrowed an old bicycle to cycle into the city as there was no snow and the road was passable, except for a 2-mile sandy stretch through the pines where I had to walk. I stayed two nights at the Windsor Hotel and took Percy Tabernacle to dinner. He was my friend in Winnipeg and had moved to Prince Albert where he ran the Central Garage Repair Shop on 13th Street but had had bad luck and bad health for months. In the evening I went to the Empress Theatre to see the Summer Stock Company in 'Lord Chumley', an old Broadway play put on as part of their summer stock programme. The 3-hour return journey to Steep Creek the next afternoon, partially in moonlight, on a saddle without springs left me very saddle-sore.

By mid-November when the temperature fell to 18 degrees below zero, I had still not received my winter kit from Winnipeg. The ice was forming across the river and so we had to move the scow onto the beach until the river had completely frozen over. With 'snow-ice' floes coming down the river the water level sometimes rose 4 or 5 feet in as many minutes until an ice-jam broke downstream.

Mr Cozens gave me and Mrs Keith, the lady book-keeper at the gold dredge 2 miles away, a lift to the city in his horse-drawn wagon box mounted on runners with no springs. To escape the head-wind on the long drive Mrs K and I lay side by side in the box with straw both beneath and on top of us! After a while, fearing that my feet were freezing, I got out and ran behind, hanging onto the sledge until Mrs Keith called out that my cheeks were freezing, so I got back under the straw. At Prince Albert I reported to Creighton who told me to stay in town until Mitchell arrived from Toronto.

Having a whole day on my hands I inspected and bought four 25 ft plots of land, one of them a corner plot, in Block 60 near the CNR track at the West end of the city, for $175.00 each. Many years later I stopped paying the taxes or rates on these properties, thus allowing their ownership to lapse to the city. Likewise, I lost plots in Edson and close to Winnipeg. The country-wide boom in real estate had infected me and swallowed most of my savings.

When Mitchell arrived he, Creighton and I drove down to the river to discuss progress, ending with a discussion with Mr Brooks on the gold dredge as to the exact location of 'La Colle Falls' which he believed were known as Big Stone rapids. I was astonished that, after two years of work, there was a complete lack of river surveys and still doubt about the topography of the river and the rapids.

When the ice had become about 12 inches thick later in the month, we hired Adam Grela's oxen to haul the boiler, engine and drilling equipment to the middle of the river again and, setting the boiler on two planks, we raised steam in it. Another week's drilling gave no hope of a suitable site for a dam and so, after the 2 months I had spent on the project, my firm, withdrew their support and my services from this ill-conceived project. Instead we recommended that the City built an extension of their existing steam power plant. Our recommendation was ignored, and I stayed on until 12ᵗʰ December when I was replaced by O.L. Flanagan, a likeable chap from the City Engineers department.

The Prince Albert engineers, together with their Toronto consultants, continued with the construction of a dam at La Colle Falls for a further two years, eventually spending $3 million before the scheme was abandoned, nearly bankrupting the city. The SKC report, condemning both the dam site and the scheme, was not revealed to the auditors by the City Council until after the $1,000,000 original estimate for the entire scheme had been exceeded and the dam only half-completed. The outbreak of the 1914 War prevented the raising of more capital and Prince Albert was the first town in the West to default in payment of interest on its bonds. Today the dam sits decaying and incomplete, stretching about a third of the way across the North Saskatchewan River.

The La Colle Falls dam was left unfinished in 1916 and as it remains today (below)

When I left Steep Creek Mr Cozens took me to Prince Albert where I caught the train to Winnipeg. There was little to see from the train and the tedium of the long journey was relieved by an interesting conversation with a very young North West Mounted Police (NWMP) constable stationed at Wadena. He had charge of a district of 3,600 sq. miles where the magistrates were not very literate and one could not even write, so he often had to act as magistrate's clerk and advise on punishment. One man, charged with stealing a boat on a small lake, had been found guilty by the local magistrate who looked through the criminal code for the correct penalty. He couldn't find 'stealing' but because 'piracy' was described as 'robbery on the high seas' he found him guilty of that. However, the penalty 'death' made him write to the Minister of Justice at Regina for advice. The courteous reply told him that he should have looked under 'theft' and that, as the man had already been held in custody for a few days, he could be released at once! It was nice to see that, on his arrival at the Wadena depot, the young constable got a hearty welcome from the usual crowd waiting for the one train a day to arrive at the station.

My Last Hunting Trip in Manitoba – December 1911

Before my job in Saskatchewan ended, Chace wrote to me offering me a job in Portland, Oregon. I made some enquiries and learned that the assignment might not last long as the project was likely to be taken over and finished by the powerful Harriman business empire, built up by the railroad baron E.H. Harriman and his son, senator Averell Harriman. I decided to decline the offer and instead to return to England and see my parents, having saved enough to pay my fare and return to Canada in the spring.

In the interval between arriving in Winnipeg and leaving for home, I managed to 'escape' into the wilderness for my last big game hunt in Manitoba. Going out by train to my old base, Lac due Bonnet and its wooden hotel, I met Mac, who was still employed by the City of Winnipeg, and also Arthur Mitchell. We fixed up a plan for a 2-day hunting trip at Boggy Creek some

10 miles along our railway where there was a telephone 'booth' containing a stove and table for the emergency use of any linesman wanting shelter.

On the following morning, Mac and I left on the City train; Arthur would follow on foot. As it was one day after the official hunting season had ended, we had hidden our rifles in our blanket rolls, mine was the take-down Savage .303, and with them we travelled in a freight box-car. Although the few in the passenger car might have thought we were making a final inspection of the Transmission Line, we wanted to be as inconspicuous as possible.

We told the engine driver to stop at Boggy Creek where there was a culvert over the stream. Just before we reached it, we threw our dunnage from the box-car into the snow and then jumped down onto the track and disappeared down the embankment, hiding on the ice in the culvert until the end of the train with its passenger car had passed. Our caution was probably over-done as it was unlikely that anybody would have had his head out of the window and seen us, for the temperature was near zero.

Collecting our dunnage and taking it to the hut, we then spent part of the afternoon cutting down and hauling some tamarack trees for fuel in the sheet iron stove. Having got the stove going we followed a trail in the snow and found the camp of Sinclair, an Indian who had Arthur's rifle on loan. There was no sign of Sinclair and only a windbreak of spruce boughs canted over the remains of a fire. No food could be found but, as we were looking over his belongings, we heard a rifle shot. We followed in the direction of the sound, quite wrongly as it turned out, to intercept any animal in flight. Foolishly, we fired at partridges - unless one hit them in the head, the heavy bullet blew the bird to pieces. We evidently disturbed a moose but saw nothing of it and returned to find the Indian back at his camp. He had shot and left a moose some distance away. We went back to our hut to await Arthur Mitchell, but he didn't turn up until the next morning after we had cooked and eaten our breakfast. He had walked the 10 miles from Lac du Bonnet, followed at some distance by one of his huskies. As soon as Arthur had had a meal, we set out and after about 4 miles we found Sinclair and another Indian, Bill Arkensaw, cutting up his moose. We stopped awhile and tasted some of the moose steak grilling 'pone-assed' over the fire.

Having rested, the three of us moved on as silently as we could for an hour or two but the 'brulé' country was noisy for stalking. Eventually getting back to our hut, we cooked a good meal of fired moose heart (given to us by Sinclair) with bacon and buttered toast. As Arthur had brought no blankets Mac lent him his and we shared mine for the night.

The next day Mac decided that he would go hunting with the Indian so that Arthur and I would have a better chance than all three of us in going noiselessly through the fallen timber. However, Arthur and I failed to get sight of a moose which we had disturbed and did not get a chance to shoot, but we did see a fine buck jumping deer which I dropped and killed with my second shot. We skinned and quartered it before leaving. Arthur brought home the head that later adorned the hall of Woodgates, my home in Suffolk. When we left Woodgates I gave it to the United Services Club in East Bergholt, together with the moose head of my earlier hunt, for their club house.

That evening we invited Sinclair to sup with us in the little hut. After the meal, Arthur and he, both squatting on the floor, discussed in the Ojibway language, a small lump which Arthur had found under the skin of the deer and which he thought should bring him better luck in moose hunting. In the season just ended he had shot none because, as the squaws had told him, a moose 'had laughed at him'.

When the Indian shook his head, Arthur, in disgust, threw it out into the snow. Years later, I read in Ernest Thompson Seton's book on the 'Wild Animals of the North' that one might find a small dermoid cyst containing hair, skin and bones in about one-in-500 animals. So, putting two and two together, I imagine that Arthur thought he had found one and that it would be a 'talisman' of good luck if he carried it.

Arthur Mitchell with rifle and buck jumping deer

Taking a break in the woods

Indian with his dog-team

Our guide with his gun and snow-shoes

I left Arthur and Mac after dinner and got a lift on the rail-bus from Lac du Bonnet to Pointe du Bois where I spent the night. The rail-bus service had recently commenced following the opening of the hydro-power plant in October. There was still no road between Lac du Bonnet and Pointe du Bois; one was not built until 1950. I went to the Powerhouse to see the five turbine-generators, which had just been commissioned; they were running perfectly generating 100,000 HP and transmitting electricity over our new line to Winnipeg. The Powerhouse had been designed to accommodate a total of 16 units which were progressively installed over the next few years, culminating in 1926 when the total generating capacity was 70 MW. The Powerhouse is still running today and is the oldest of Manitoba Hydro's generating stations.

The original turbine-generators in the Pointe du Bois Powerhouse

Home to England in January and Return to Canada in March 1912

There was a lot to do during the three hectic days in Winnipeg before I left the city and headed homewards. I said good-bye to Chace who was leaving for the Portland, Oregon, job himself and I had several hours in Dr Curry's dentist's chair, costing me $100 for some long over-due dental work. I entertained Pearson, Evans and the Coombes to dinner at the Royal Alexandra Hotel and went to the Deanery for a Christmas party, playing Santa Claus for the Mossman children. It was Christmas Eve by the time I caught the Eastern Express for Montreal, arriving there on Boxing Day. I booked in for two nights in the Windsor Hotel and called on my Montreal pals, including Bernard Collett and the Rose family, before catching the CPR boat-train to St John's, New Brunswick, where I boarded the 'Empress of Britain' for the voyage back to Liverpool.

During the 10 weeks following my arrival in England on January 6th, I travelled the country and saw all my family and friends, catching up with their news, telling them of my adventures and showing them my photographs of Canada. First stop was of course The Place at Gt. Wenham to stay with my parents who had moved back there from Dorchester in 1910. I based myself there for the first month and also for the last 3 weeks before I returned to Canada. Life in Wenham was the same as ever; walks around the farm with Father, visits to the aunts at the Hill House and to other friends and relations nearby, bridge and music in the evenings, church on Sundays with my aunts and sisters in the choir and me at the organ, and trips to Flatford with sisters Clara and May and cousin Katie Sears to skate on the ice in the fields which had been flooded for the purpose.

In London for a few days in February I visited Mrs Atkins in Herne Hill, Mrs Skinner and Cyril in the Boltons and Cyril (now Dr) Day in Hammersmith. Mrs Skinner was her usual charming and generous self and took us to a performance of 'Louise',

Charpentier's '*roman musical*', at Hammerstein's New London Opera House in Kingsway which had opened in November. She also took us to 'Nightbirds', a musical comedy by Johann Strauss, at the Lyric Theatre, where it had been first performed in December. On February 6th I was in the Strand to see Queen Alexandra and Princess Victoria in advance of the main procession on their way to the State Thanksgiving at St Paul's. I had a close up view of King George V, Queen Mary, the Prince of Wales and Princess Mary in their carriage which drew up nearby for a presentation from the Westminster Council.

For three weeks in February I toured the country by train to see my brother Charles in Sheffield, old friends in Rotherham, Gainsborough, Liverpool and Rock Ferry, and finally my brother English in Barry where he was Prior of the Order of St Paul's, Welsh branch, working amongst destitute seamen.

Return with Cyril Skinner and Search for a Job

During my visit to London to see Mrs Skinner, she had asked if I would take Cyril with me as my 'ward' when I returned to Canada, show him around and help him find a job, offering to pay me £100 plus expenses. He had recently graduated in Engineering from Cambridge and, of course, I was delighted for him to join me. We left Liverpool on March 15th in the S.S. Victorian, sharing a cabin and both succumbing to seasickness in the rough seas. It was so bad that not until the fifth day out was I able to eat my first meal in the saloon!

We had 20 hours in Halifax harbour, enabling us to see the town under snow conditions, and finally disembarked at St John's, New Brunswick, where we started our sightseeing tour as Cyril's mother had planned. I introduced Cyril to my friends as we went round the cities of Montreal (4 days), Ottawa and Toronto where we were lucky to find the ice on Toronto Bay just good enough for a sail in an ice-yacht on April 1st. We spent two days at Niagara seeing the usual sights and I arranged a conducted tour of the two great hydro-electric powerhouses of the Niagara Falls Power Co. and the Ontario Power Co.

On April 3rd we left Toronto on the train to Winnipeg, passing Lake Superior which was still frozen; the first time for years that it had been completely frozen over. With Winnipeg as our base, I took Cyril to see the projects on which I had worked - the Red River Bridge and the St Andrew's Dam. Then we took the train to Lac du Bonnet and checked in to the small hotel there – rather different from the Royal Alexandra Hotel where we had stayed in Winnipeg. The next morning I borrowed Mac McGibbon's speeder and we 'jiggered', sitting side by side on a board, all the way to Pointe du Bois, getting off to walk up the steeper grades and stopping at Bear Creek Spring for a break. We saw the Transmission Line on the way and looked over the Powerhouse at Pointe du Bois where I showed Cyril some of the drawings before we turned in.

Cyril and I jigger from Lac du Bonnet to Point du Bois. April 10. 1912 28. miles

Cyril and I jigger the 28 miles from Lac du Bonnet to Pointe du Bois

Back in Winnipeg we took a room at the more modest La Claire Hotel and both started looking for work. After a week working as a repairman at the Consolidated Motor & Bicycle shop, which he found totally unsatisfactory, Cyril accepted a job as a rodman on the survey for a small hydro-plant and left Winnipeg for Dryden, Ontario. He would not allow me to supplement his $40 a month pay with money from the £800 per year 'trust' fund I had been authorised by his mother to give him; refusing to be a 'remittance man' he tore up my cheques and preferred to live on his small pay.

Before he left we heard the terrible news of the sinking of the SS Titanic, the White Star Liner which was the largest in the world with a displacement of 66,000 tons. It sank on April 15th within a few hours of striking an iceberg on her maiden voyage, with the loss of 1,595 lives, including Col. J.J. Astor (thought to be the richest man in the world worth $87 million), Isidor Straus (co-owner of Macy's) and other millionaires. Only about 800 passengers were rescued by the Carpathia, including J Bruce Ismay, the Chairman of the White Star Line, who jumped into a lifeboat with the women and children; he became known as 'the Coward of the Titanic' and 'the most hated man in the world'.

The search for a job for myself was becoming urgent and was the focus of most of my time and efforts. I contacted all the companies I had worked for, the senior engineers I knew and wrote numerous letters to the engineering heads of companies such as the CPR, CNR, GTP and Hudson Bay Railway companies, Westinghouse and similar equipment manufacturers, Dominion Bridge Company and other contractors, consulting engineering firms and the City Engineering and Power departments of Winnipeg, Toronto and Montreal. None of these organisations seemed to have any vacancies and I declined the only offer I received of $100 a month 'for the season' from F.A. Creighton at Prince Albert; it was too short term and the pay was not enough.

During my stay in Winnipeg I also refused an offer of $1,200 for the 4 building plots I had bought in Prince Albert for $700. This turned out to be a bad mistake as, years later, I tore up the deeds having given up paying the annual rates as a bad spec.

The Sinking of the Titanic
15th April 1912

Main Street, Winnipeg, circa 1912

The Drawing Room at the Royal Alexandra Hotel, Winnipeg

When not job hunting and visiting possible employers I had many social contacts, meeting up regularly with Pearson, McGibbon, Clendenning, Geoff Lawson, the Taylors as well as other friends and colleagues. We would go for walks, have long talks in our rooms and go for lunch or tea at Eaton's. In the evenings we went to 'moving picture shows' or to the Orpheum or the Walker or Empress Theatres followed by supper at the Olympia Café. We saw Bernard Shaw's play 'You Never Can Tell' and the famous English actor, William Faversham, in 'The Farm', as well as Tiller's Sunshine Girls.

WINNIPEG STORE OF THE T. EATON CO. LIMITED

But the largest part of my spare time was spent with the Coombes at the Deanery, and particularly with Marjorie, of whom I had become very fond. I often took her out to the theatre and to dinners in town and sometimes Pearson would join us with his girl, Peggy Beck who was also a friend of Marjorie. In June I went to the annual Horse Show, 'a brilliant society event', and chatted to Marjorie and her mother who were in the Lieut. Governor (D.C. Cameron)'s box; they were well connected in Winnipeg society.

Some afternoons I spent in the Carnegie Library brushing up my technical knowledge and reading about the geology of Canada which interested me and which I thought might be useful in some future job.

During the warm early summer weather I could not resist going back to Lac du Bonnet for a couple of weekends canoeing on the Winnipeg River with Mac. On one these trips we took three ladies out to a party in a 16-foot canoe – it was a very live weight of 800lbs and my diary says that 'had our guests been cool-headed men, it would have been much more enjoyable!' - but we got back safely.

By mid-June, having spent practically all my remaining capital, I was desperate to find work. I had had no luck in Winnipeg and so decided to follow up two possible jobs back in Montreal and call on firms to whom I had written with details of my experience. Before leaving I made the 210 miles train journey to Dryden to see Cyril Skinner. He had settled in well and did not need any particular help from me, but we agreed to keep in touch regularly by letter. Back in Winnipeg I went to the Deanery to say goodbye to Marjorie and her parents and called on Pearson and the Taylors before boarding a practically empty CPR Pullman car for the 1,500 mile journey to Montreal. We passed the 'jackfish' (the northern pike) country along the north shore of Lake Superior in daylight and had a short stop in Ottawa, just time enough to see the Parliament Buildings, before arriving in Montreal at 7 pm on 18th June, where I found Arthur Atkins waiting at the station to meet me.

Resident Engineer with T Pringle & Son - Montreal – June 1912

After a night in the Welland Hotel I found a room at 630 Dorchester West where I left my baggage and went straight to the offices of T. Pringle & Son, a firm of consulting engineers to whom I had written on spec. Mr Costigan, the Vice-President, was not there but I was told to return the next morning when Mr Guy Wynn would see me. To my surprise when I arrived, he said that he had telegraphed me at my Winnipeg address only the evening before to offer me a job and asked me to start with them right away!

So, after a quick lunch and change I started work that very afternoon, at $125.00 a month, as the Resident Engineer on the construction of a new plant for Canadian Steel Foundries at Longue Pointe. The project consisted of a series of factory buildings with a large office block, the top floor of which was a room, without any supporting columns, to be used for laying out full size templates of railway points on the floor.

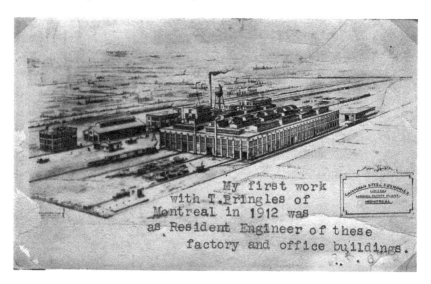

Canadian Steel Foundries – Longue Pointe, Montreal

For the next two months, July and August, my job was to supervise the building contractors and to check the quality of their work, from the integrity of the water and sewer pipework underground to the melting point of the pitch they were using to seal the roof. It was the height of summer and I found the temperature and humidity 'hellish' as I clambered around the site, up and down scaffolding, so that most evenings I returned to my room tired out.

My work on the Longue Pointe project finished in August and I was given a short job, at a few hours' notice, by Costigan who asked me to go to Sherbrooke from where I took the 'dusty, dirty, rocky train of the Quebec Central Railway' to Thetford Mines, the centre of the world's largest asbestos-producing region after asbestos was discovered there in 1876. My job was to obtain data from the manager of the Bell Asbestos Company for a proposed concrete-arch bridge across the river there. After reporting back to Costigan, I left Montreal once more, this time on aboard 'a most luxuriously equipped boat' on the St Lawrence to go to Trois-Rivieres for my next assignment.

Survey for Hydro-electric Scheme on St Maurice River – August 1912

I was really looking forward to this assignment which involved carrying out a survey for a hydro-electric power scheme on the St Maurice River between Grandes-Piles and Les Petites-Piles. Not only did I enjoy working in the back woods of Canada but the salary I had been offered, with an increase of $50 to $175.00 a month, was most welcome.

Settlers had been attracted to Grandes-Piles in the 1850's by the large stands of white and red pine and the village became the gateway to lumberjacks and log drivers. A sawmill was built there in 1878 and the railway from Trois-Rivieres followed. The pulp and paper industry in the area was expanding and with it the demand for electricity. Our new scheme was primarily required to supply the Wayagamack Pulp & Paper Co. at whose head offices in Trois Rivieres I met Frank Ritchie and C.R. Whitehead, the President. Whitehead was our ultimate client; he was a prominent financier and owner of the Wayagamack company as well as the Wabasso Cotton Mill. He took me to meet M. Berlinguet, the District Engineer, in whose offices we were able to examine all the information he had on the St Maurice River.

The Sanatorium Hotel in Trois-Rivieres was my base for a couple of days before I went by train to Grand-Mere and was driven down the steepest of hills to Petites-Piles where board and lodging was provided in the home of a French-Canadian Government foreman; it was indescribably dirty and crude, but we could not complain as it was the only place available and we had begged him to give us rooms.

In Petites-Piles I joined A.W. Gregory and we started our work of surveying the riverbed and its surroundings. After some difficulty in finding suitable assistance I employed Paul and Philippe, two non-English speaking French Canadians, and one John Smith to act as rod and chain men and help me with the survey. We dug

138

test pits and laid out a 1,000 ft traverse line on the west shore but found the precipitous cliffs of rock difficult to chain and sight round with the transit level. We also took soundings along lines across the river below Petites-Piles using a scow.

In order to investigate the nature of the river bottom, I sent for a diver from Montreal. He arrived on the job at the same time as I received a letter from my chief who wrote 'We are sending you John Millen, the best-known diver around. You should treat him gently as he has just come out of prison for pulling a man's ear off!'

To gain a better understanding of the river bottom myself, I used his diving suit in several descents to a depth of 30 feet, in a current of about 3 feet per second. When I reached the bottom and before leaving the ladder, I tied to its foot a long cord to enable me to find my way back in the utter darkness. The water, although 'clear', was yellow in colour from the muskeg upstream. Groping around on the bottom I satisfied myself as to the presence of a ledge of bedrock, however, due to my inexperience with the valve in the suit above my head, I suffered great pain in my ears which lasted for some weeks afterwards.

Using a transit level during the survey of the St Maurice River

Putting on my diving suit

Ready for the dive

We were diving off the scow in the middle of the river and once, when we were working just upstream of the Grandes-Piles Falls, I calculated that the mooring rope we were using from the scow to the shore might not be strong enough; if it broke the scow would be swept over the falls, so we made additional arrangements to secure it to the shore. The rope did break, and my prediction so impressed the professional diver, whose life and that of myself and the others on the scow had probably been saved, that he offered me a partnership in his business, more remunerative than engineering. Knowing his recent past, I decided not to accept his offer!

For nearly a fortnight, I had the further assistance of Thomas Beagley, a young McGill University graduate. He helped me to take lines of levels from which I produced contour maps of the district. However, he did not enjoy the rough living and daily soaking to the waist and found his first adventures in a canoe on a river in which logs were floating on their way to the pulp and paper mills, much more hazardous than he anticipated or liked.

Every year millions of logs were driven down the St Maurice River to the pulp mills. Walking on the logs, without stopping on any one of them, was dangerous but it was the only way of taking a line of levels to a Government 'benchmark' two miles upstream. One Sunday afternoon we walked the 2 miles from Petites-Piles to Grand-Mere in the centre of the river on the log-boom, assisted only once by a motor-boat to cross a particularly dangerous spot. After supper at the Laurentide Inn we went to a service at St Stephen's Church before our hour's walk home in the moonlight.

Logs on their way to pulp and paper mills

Beagley left at the end of September and G.R. Heckle, from Ambursens Hydraulic Construction Co, came with my boss Wynn

141

to look over the site and examine our survey results in order to decide on the most suitable location for a dam. They agreed that my proposed site was the most favourable and that I should return to Montreal to prepare an estimate for the project. Our journey back to the city was magnificent with the woods in their Fall colours; the silver birches, the scarlet-leaved maples and the dark cedars made the countryside look like a fairyland.

Design Engineering and Life in Montreal 1912 -1914

My return to the city marked the beginning of a two-year spell of engineering design in Pringles' offices, beginning with the St Maurice River hydro-electric scheme based upon my selected site for the dam. Ambursens quoted $500,000 for the construction of a dam of their hollow type and I worked this into our estimate for the whole project which came to a total of $2½ million. Wynn and I went to Trois Rivieres to discuss the estimate with Whitehead, the project promoter. He entertained us to lunch in his 150 year-old home and then took us on a 7 mile covered sleigh ride to inspect another possible site for a hydro-electric power scheme at Les Forges Rapids. There we saw natural gas bubbling up through the half-melted snow and were intrigued by the possibility of tapping it for a gas heater if one ever camped there! In 1924 this site saw the construction of the La Gabelle hydro-electric scheme, eight years after our scheme at Grandes-Piles was commissioned. Eventually a total of nine hydro-electric schemes were built on the St Maurice River.

Unknown to me, my work on and in the St Maurice River had been watched closely by one of Whitehead's forest engineers. It had impressed him to such an extent that years later Whitehead became a personal friend and offered me two appointments. The first, in 1915, was to become the General Manager of the St Maurice River Log Driving and Book Association, whose role was to assist, with lumbermen and amphibian craft called 'alligators', the 10 million logs floated down the river each year to reach the pulp mills near the mouth of the river where it joined the St

Lawrence. The second offer in September 1926 was to manage his property on Anticosti Island. I turned down both offers for different reasons; the first came when I was an officer in the British Army in France and the second when I was enjoying being back in London after almost 20 years abroad and had a job which still gave me plenty of opportunity for international travel.

My next project was the design of an 8-storey building in reinforced concrete with brick facing required as a machinery warehouse for Canadian Fairbanks Morse Co, near Windsor Station in Montreal. This involved a 'flat-slab' design with minimum supporting beams and girders in the floors, and concrete columns and footings to support a load of 300-600,000 pounds. To acquire the necessary up-to-date knowledge, I took a post-graduate course in the evenings given by Prof. Brown at McGill University. Only in Canada in those early days would an English graduate in *Electrical* Engineering be given an 8-storey warehouse to design! It took me almost 3 months, until Christmas, to complete the design calculations and the draughting work involved; draughting was not my strong point and I found it neither easy nor enjoyable.

When I returned from the St Maurice project in September, I moved into rooms at 4265 St Catherine Street West where Robert Holmes, a colleague from Pringles was living; he later became a friend and one of my regular companions. John D. Crichton, another work colleague, joined us later in the year. All such rooms in boarding houses were only bed-sitters and we had to eat all our meals out. However, when our landlady, Miss Pipe, went on

Canadian Fairbanks Morse Building

143

holiday she left me in charge and in exchange gave me free run of her kitchen so that I was at least able to prepare breakfast there.

St Catherine's Street, Montreal

Few of my bachelor friends from my first year in the city (1907/8) were still around, having either married or moved on, and so for the first few months I spent most of my evenings after work alone. Harry Cutmore, his wife, and daughter Ella, who was now 12 years old, were still in town and gave me a warm welcome and a home cooked dinner from time to time. I used to go round to their apartment for dinner and music and they invited me to spend Christmas Day with them, putting on a gorgeous feast followed by music and songs after supper. To repay their hospitality I took them to the theatre; we saw a performance of 'The Pink Lady' at His Majesty's Theatre, 'Elijah' staged as a grand opera, and Grace George acting in Compton McKenzie's adaptation of his novel 'Carnival' in which he played the male lead himself.

Mr and Mrs J.C. Rose, to whom Bernard Collett had introduced me, were also still around and invited me to their home occasionally; Mr Rose also gave me lunch at the Engineers Club sometimes to introduce me to some of his friends and colleagues. My cousin Arthur Atkins returned to Montreal in November and my brother's friend, Charles W. Parry and his wife, emigrated a few months later; we used to meet up for lunch or supper at Cooper's or the Edinburgh Café and sometimes I would take a street-car to their home at 726 Avenue Champagneur for the evening. However, my most interesting and elegant evenings out were spent at Mrs Gnaedinger's whom I had met on board ship returning to England in 1909. We had kept in touch and she used to invite me to join her and a few other friends for bridge or musical soirées at which a light supper of anchovy toast and cheese and biscuits was served.

My habit of rising early, first acquired during my job in the Gainsborough engineering works, used to make me feel lazy in the evenings. I was always up by 6 am and in the evenings, after a day's work I was fagged out, frequently going to a moving picture show after dinner to relax, my daily ration of energy exhausted. Even at the time of writing these memoirs at the end of my 8th decade, I am still unable to stay in bed after 6 am with breakfast generally over by 6.15 am.

Another habit which had stayed with me since College days was the careful control and recording of all my expenditure. My daily living expenses were very modest, amounting to little more than $1 a day for breakfast (25c), lunch (30c), dinner (30c) and late supper (10c), plus a paper (5c) and a moving picture show (10c). To these were sometimes added laundry (55c), haircut (20c), shoeshine (10c), pressing and repair of suit and overcoat ($1.25) and new clothes such as shirts ($1), boots ($7) and a new suit ($32). All detailed and noted in my diary! As a change from this frugal fare in December, I paid $5 to attend the annual dinner of the Quebec Fish and Game Protection Association at which the excellent menu included green turtle soup, partridge, caribou and plover!

My salary and bonus, together with my economical lifestyle, enabled me to save about $400 during the year so that by the end of 1913 I had a total of $881 in cash and my bank account.

Having a little more spending power after my salary rise, I decided to insure myself for $5,000 with the Employers Liability Insurance Co. and took out a policy which would pay me $25 a week in the event of loss of earnings due to disablement, accident or illness. In one of my regular letters home I told my brother Charles that I had nominated him as the beneficiary of the policy in the event of my death.

Writing letters was one of my most regular and pleasant evening occupations. Not only did I keep in frequent touch with all the members of my family back home, but I also wrote regularly to Arthur Barnard and Aunt Agnes in British Columbia and to the friends I had made in Toronto, Winnipeg and Lac du Bonnet as well as those from my days at Marshalls in Gainsborough, some of whom had also emigrated to Canada.

I had been elected an Associate Member of the Canadian Society of Civil Engineers and, as part of my professional development, I went to their library and reading room in my spare time to keep up-to-date with the latest technology, study papers and attend lectures on the design of hydro-electric plant, reinforced concrete structures, the use of cement guns to coat steelwork for fire protection and other such developments. It was also a good place to read the Illustrated London News and write my weekly letters home.

During my first year in Montreal I had enjoyed a lot of ice-skating and tobogganing but had never tried skiing, so this year (1913) in January I joined Alec Miller, John Pearson and Eric Billington, a graduate at McGill University and incidentally their star football player, for my first skiing weekend. We went to Lachute where there were gentle slopes for beginners and spent the day amongst many other novices finding our ski-legs and getting badly bruised! I had also taken my rifle and automatic revolver and the four of us had some shooting practice at targets in the woods, rather more successfully.

My first attempt at skiing – in the Laurentians near Lachute

My first attempt   Jan. 5. 13.

On Sundays I practised my skiing on the steeper slopes of Mount Royal, once finishing with an uncontrolled non-stop run downhill into Sherbrooke Street, the Park Lane of Montreal, on the way back to my digs. Fortunately, there was little traffic and no policemen around to apprehend me.

Having become more proficient I went with my friends on a skiing weekend to Mont Tremblant, the highest point in the Laurentians north of Montreal. We skied from Lac Mercier to Lac Tremblant and were the only humans in sight on the slopes that are now, 45 years later, crowded with Montrealers who pack the special weekend ski-trains.

Meanwhile my design assignments at Pringles had become quite varied and included two more reinforced concrete buildings; a 5-storey warehouse for the Parker Foundry Co. and a 4-storey building for the Dominion Textile Co; new buildings for the Canadian Wire Co. and the Wabasso Cotton Mill and screw conveyors to handle 5 tons/hour of sludge from the Alkali house for the Wayagamack Pulp & Paper Co.

Then in February, Wynn asked me to go with him to Magog, to the Dominion Textile Company's works, where I was to stand in for E.C. Leete as Resident Engineer for a few weeks on a new one-storey weave shed for the Magog Cotton Mill. It was 505 feet long and 91½ feet wide. A special wood floor, 46,000 square feet, was constructed of polished maple wood strips, laid on Hemlock planking, as the foundation for the new automatic looms, which were to be driven from 8 lines of shafting.

Wynn and I took rooms at Battle's House (now a tourist hotel) located in a beautiful position on the shore of Lake Memphremagog and I spent a month there inspecting the progress of the building work and testing the generators in the hydro-power plant 3 miles down-river. My services as pianist and accompanist were once again in demand after dinner to entertain some of the hotel guests as well as a few locals from the small town.

One Sunday just before my assignment in Magog ended in mid-March, I took two English lads from the Mill for a climb to the top of Mt Orford. We set off on snowshoes at 10 am in fine weather and reached the 3,000 ft summit by about 2.30 pm. However, the descent was more of an adventure as we were caught by a strong wind and blinding snow blizzard which reduced the visibility to nil so that we could not see the rocky path down. We did eventually get down safely and walked the 7 miles back through the blizzard to the welcome warmth of the hotel fires.

The vagaries of the March weather produced temperatures in Montreal of up to 35 deg. On the same day that Prince Albert in Saskatchewan registered 22 deg. below zero and Winnipeg -2 deg, Montreal was a warm 22 deg. That month I first met J.M. Crabbe, an emigrant from Scotland, who joined me at T Pringle & Son. Our friendship lasted until his death in 1958 and resulted in my being introduced by him to Balfour Beatty & Co with whom I worked from 1924 until my retirement 31 years later in 1955.

Alone in the evenings and sometimes on Saturday afternoons, I would go as many as three or four times a week to a theatre to see a play (50 cents) or more often a moving picture show (10 cents), often coming away from the movies frustrated with myself at the 'complete waste of time'! In those days, films were short, black-and-white and silent, except for a continuous piano accompaniment until 1913 when the principal cinemas started installing a 'unit orchestra' or organ. The music which was played was often quite monotonous unless the organist was particularly talented, which a few of them were. Films varied from popular stories such as 'Tess of the d'Urbervilles' to a documentary on Scott's ill-fated expedition to the Antarctic which was particularly moving. Recent releases were also popular: 'Her Nephews from Labrador', was an American film which had premiered in January and 'Rainey's African Hunt' (1912) went on to become the most successful movie of the decade. It was a blockbuster movie about a wealthy playboy and big game hunter, which had been heralded as 'serious entertainment for wealthy people at top prices' when it opened on Broadway, to distinguish it from the fiction films commonly favoured! However, it was also silent, and it was not until May that I saw my first talking picture as soon they came out.

149

Some venues presented films as part of an evening of vaudeville or cabaret performances accompanied by live music. Crichton and I first experienced one of these shows in April when we had supper at Kastels. During the meal we were entertained to a cabaret with the dancing girls coming to our table, singing and playing the violin. It was more fun for a couple of bachelors than our dinners of 'planked steak' at Krausmann's and I went back on my own a few days later after treating myself to a dinner of salmon mayonnaise followed by strawberries and cream at the Ratskeller.

During the hot summer weather my favourite way to spend Sundays was with my canoe 'Salvo' starting from the Cartierville Canoe Club, of which I was a member, and paddling a few miles up the Back River for picnics, practicing with my .22 rifle, or watching birds through field glasses and swimming in the clear cold water. In those days, the river was completely unspoiled; the banks were covered with virgin forest and the tiny islands, now submerged, on which we landed to swim and to light a fire, cook our al fresco meals of sausages and tomatoes or bacon and eggs with fruit and cream to follow, and sometimes to camp for the night, were uninhabited.

Perhaps the most memorable of many such delightful weekends was one with Holmes and J.F. Stein when we canoed from Cartierville up to the Lake of the Two Mountains. A gale of wind and rain spoilt our night out in the open for we had not taken a tent with us; it also made our return across the corner of the lake the next day extremely hazardous. The big waves, which were at right angles to our route, forced us to paddle back and forth, each time gaining a few feet until we reached the mouth of the river. From there we tried to canoe around l'Ile Bizard, but the wind was too strong, and we had to turn back and take the more exciting alternative of shooting the German Rapids. We eventually arrived at Cat Island ready to relax over a camp supper.

To return hospitality which I had received as a lone bachelor, I entertained a small party of ladies to tea at the newly opened, and super-luxurious, Ritz-Carlton Hotel on Sherbrooke Street and then took my guests for a drive to the top of Mount Royal in a horse-drawn Victoria. I entertained Marjorie Coombes in a similar way one Sunday when she came to Montreal for a weekend in June – we spent two or three hours together and I then went on to Mrs Gnaedinger's for supper and some music before returning to my room at 9.30 pm.

My canoe 'Salvo' with two friends Frank de Jong and J F Stein

Camping on Strawberry Island during a canoe trip

Although economic growth remained strong in central and western Canada up to the start of the War in 1914, in Quebec and the Eastern Provinces the economy slowed in 1913 and capital ceased to come from England. The shortage of money made the harvest that year particularly important. Wynn became depressed by the slump in the stock market in May; shares in CPR and Wayagamack were down and Pringles were finding it more difficult to get new work. Fortunately, I was still working on the details of the Canadian Fairbanks Morse building on which Crabbe had been appointed our Resident Engineer. I often spent the day there helping him with various measuring and setting out jobs and we would have lunch together at Windsor Station. The office was very slack and had it not been for that job I would have had little to do.

Robert Holmes, however, was anything but depressed; he had gone to Quebec City on Tuesday 3rd June and returned a couple of days later with Miss Sarah Weatherhead who had just arrived in Canada and whom he married at 8.15 am that Saturday morning 7th June! And so I lost another of my bachelor friends!

Similarly, Geoff Lawson who had been one of our group in Winnipeg, arrived in Montreal to stay with me for a few nights in July before going on to Quebec to meet Miss Mabel Simmons off the boat. He returned with her to Montreal and they were married a few days later in the Church of St James the Apostle, followed by a blessing from Father Donnelly at St Patrick's. They entertained me to dinner that evening and afterwards I took them to a show at the Imperial Theatre. I had known Geoff for years since he was an apprentice at the Foundry in Dorchester where he had been a lodger in my parents' house before emigrating to Canada. Yerbury, with whom I was at school in Dorchester, was also now working in Montreal, as were several of my year from the Central Technical College. 1913 was one of the peak years for English emigration to Canada.

Other arrivals in Quebec that summer included Mrs Skinner who came to meet Cyril and tour parts of Canada with him, and my cousin Ada Atkins, whom I met off the 'Tunisian'. I escorted her to the YWCA, took her to the bank to get some money and the next day saw her onto her train to Winnipeg en route to the small village of Marquis in Saskatchewan.

All of us young engineers used to compare our salaries and keep an eye out for better opportunities, so I was rather upset when D.A. Evans told me that he was getting $230 a month working in the Transcontinental Railway Shops. However, the feeling did not last long and I was very pleasantly surprised when I received a bonus of $175 (one month's salary) a few days later. At the end of the month I was even more surprised to receive a telegram from David Gilmore in New York: 'Leaving for Chile in two weeks - am interested in your application – what are the terms of your present engagement – wire collect'. I replied: 'Would accept three thousand a year plus living and transportation expenses – could leave in 10 days – writing tonight', knowing that it was unlikely to be accepted. I was enjoying my work with Pringles and was only interested in moving if the pay was significantly higher.

My design and survey work during the year included a new factory near Montreal for the Canadian Wire Company; roof trusses for a laboratory at the new Dominion Arsenal; under-silt foundations for Vickers new ship building yard on ground just reclaimed from the St Lawrence and a steel-framed general stores building for Canadian Vickers Ltd.

Incidentally, this last building had fireproof floors of an entirely new construction. The material, a mixture of wood shavings and plaster-of-Paris, was poured around a system of wires (not steel rods) strung between the steel beams, the ends being hooked on to the flanges, thus acting as a suspension system. Before adopting this system, we carried out a practical test on its load bearing capacity and resistance to a very hot fire.

I also carried out an investigation into the stability of the large, stone-built factory buildings of the Valleyfield Cotton Mills.

Examinations of the safety and stability of buildings were required where new structures had been built on old walls. In one case, a large water tank had been installed, for fire protection, on a downtown office building. I concluded that the only forces which appeared to be preventing its collapse were the 'force of habit and the grace of God'.

As winter approached and the mosquitoes disappeared, I set up a camp bed on the balcony of my bedsit so that I could sleep outdoors, even sometimes in temperatures below zero Fahrenheit. The whole bundle of my blankets and rabbit skin sleeping bag spent the days against the hot radiator in my room, so that going outside with it to bed at night required no effort of will. In the morning, or during the night if falling snow tickled my face and woke me, I picked up my bed roll and brought it into the warm room. I also did this when I had visitors, such as Crabbe, who sometimes stayed in my room (and slept in my bed) after we had been out for the evening. I was not alone in this practice and some Montrealers who had balconies did the same.

Possibly as a result of my growing agnosticism, my habit of attending a church service every Sunday had taken a back seat to my other weekend activities, skating and skiing in winter and canoeing in summer. However, I did go to one service to hear Dr Paterson Smyth preach; ironically his sermon was on 'Doubters'! I also attended concerts whenever I could and was lucky to get a ticket to the concert at the Arena at which Nellie Melba, the famous Australian soprano, Jan Kubelik, the Czech violinist and Edmund Burke, the Canadian baritone, were performing during their 'sold-out' tour of Canada and the US. A very beautiful gramophone recording of Dame Nellie Melba singing 'Ave Maria' can still be bought.

To keep my own music skills up to date I hired a piano for $6 a month and practised for an hour or so after work, playing Rachmaninov, Beethoven sonatas or Chopin etudes, and of course playing for friends who came round for 'some music' in the evenings.

The last liner of the season docked in Montreal on 26th November 1913 and the last mail steamer left that day, although ice had not yet formed on the St Lawrence. Sailings during the winter months normally started and finished in Quebec City or St John's. December was cold and there was a particularly heavy snowfall on Christmas Eve when a record 17 inches fell overnight.

The Cutmores were always very hospitable and welcomed me any time for tea, dinner and an evening of music and conversation. In February 1914, when Ella was just 15 years old, I took her over the mountain to see the Fête de Nuit and Carnival of the Park Slide Club where the illuminations, bonfire and firework display was watched by a crowd of 40,000. We also went to see the ski-jumping competitions on the mountain.

Moose Hunting in Northern Quebec

Two unsuccessful moose-hunts were my last of the kind and therefore have to be described. In December 1913, I had arranged with R.B. Manning, the Secretary of the Kiskissink Fish and Game Club, to outfit me with dog transport, food, tent, and guides for a 5-day moose hunt. The Club was 7 hours by train north of Quebec City and was the centre for outfitting rich American members for camping and fishing in the various lakes in the neighbourhood during the summer and fall.

I left Montreal on November 30th for Quebec, arriving at the Hotel Chateau Frontenac at midnight. Finding my room at 100 degrees Fahrenheit, I turned off the radiators, opened the window and lay stripped on my bed. Waking, I found the room temperature was now at freezing point and my nude body chilled which resulted in a cold.

The next day I got off the northbound train at Kiskissink near Lake St John and was met by the Club Secretary and an Indian. Supper was partridge and chicken. The following day we left with Alexan, a full-blooded Indian, Johnny and Willie (half-breeds), the Club Secretary and the two dogs, each hauling a sleigh with 150lbs of food and dunnage. The snow scarcely covered the ground causing heavy pulling by the dogs even when helped by a rare shove behind or when the sleighs were thrust aside from a rock.

We crossed one lake but, on reaching the 10-mile long one, we had to skirt the banks; even then both sleighs broke through the ice, the water spoiling some of our provisions. After pulling the sleighs by hand round a precipitous point of rock we made a fire and lunched. The dogs were then harnessed again and we progressed over ice which cracked; it was not more than 1½ inches thick but was of the reliable 'black' variety. Crossing the 1½ mile wide lake, we camped near the Little Bostonnais River. Two tents were erected by the 'breeds' and aromatic balsam boughs laid as mattresses whilst I wandered through muskegy bush for partridge. Supper was partridge.

During the night a fall of sleet and then snow changed the appearance of the world around us. The Club Secretary and Alexan having left us, Johnny and I walked down to the river and followed a portage trail. We followed the tracks of a bull moose but, after half an hour of difficult stalking, perspiring with excitement and all faculties strained, we failed. Johnny had seen the horns of the bull come up and disappear for he had sensed our approach.

We reached the Lake Margaret crossing where we camped for lunch before cutting into dense woods and walking miles to Lac des Iles. Here we saw fresh wolf tracks, otter, fox, and mink tracks. Then we came homewards across Lac Demi and Lac à la Dame. The journey back seemed endless, Johnny was tired 'au genoux' after tramping through the burnt-out woods, and the only animals or birds we saw, except the momentary glimpse of the moose, were two weasels!

'A little more snow during the night. After breakfast struck camp, loaded sleighs and with Johnny leading, testing ice thickness on the lake and cutting away fallen trees in the bush, and Willie driving the dogs, we traversed Long Lake. Then cutting our way, foot by foot, through the bush we reached a small timber dam and old log shack at noon and soon had dinner.'

December 4th: 'Whilst the boys put up my tent, supported it with balsam boughs and cut firewood, I wandered a couple of miles with my shotgun to seek rabbits or partridges. I climbed to the top of two hills and had wonderful panoramic views of lake and wilderness. An early supper.'

December 5th: 'Several degrees colder. Johnny and I start at 8 am, Willie going on his own trapping. We come across fresh moose tracks and follow them until we found that we had disturbed the after-breakfast snooze of a cow-moose. We tramp a few more miles. See a fine fresh timber-wolf track, also signs of otter, fox and rabbit. After lunch at a lakeside we go on, but I break through ice to above my knees and after taking off my boots to empty them and to wring out my socks, I walk home alone. Johnny turns up at camp 1½ hours later announcing that Willie must be lost! Saw one live animal today, almost the first except rabbits and partridges since I struck the wilderness – a grey-white bird, the size of a pigeon.'

December 7th: 'Strike camp and load the two sleighs. We make our way back to Kiskissink without adventure. Snow was falling most of the day. That evening I board the night train for Quebec arriving at 8 am. Breakfast at the great Chateau Frontenac Hotel, also lunch. During the morning, I attend a wonderful High Mass (Day of the Immaculate Conception) at the Basilica. Magnificent ceremonial with Cardinal as the central figure. Vestments, incense and music appeal to sight, nose, and ears. Reach Montreal by train, having a comfortable seat in the 'parlor' car. So ended an expensive and unsuccessful moose-hunt.'

Crossing Lake Bostonnais on a moose hunt with Indian guides

My tent supported by balsam boughs

My last moose hunt, also unsuccessful, was in 1914 just before I left Canada to join up and go to war. It will be described shortly. But before that I must recount the following story of the One Hundred Million Dollar Baby.

The One Hundred Million Dollar Baby

During dinner on the evening I arrived at the Kiskissink Club, the Secretary told me about two members of the Club, whom he had outfitted that summer.

They were Mr and Mrs (Walsh) McLean, both multi-millionaires. Evalyn Walsh McLean was a prominent Washington socialite and had inherited $10 million from her father, Thomas Walsh, the Colorado mining tycoon. Edward Beale McLean was the millionaire publisher of the 'Washington Post' of which he became the owner on the death of his father in 1916. Their only son Vinson, born in 1910, was therefore the heir to the largest fortune in America and was referred to in the press as the 'One Hundred Million Dollar Baby'.

Apparently, they arrived at the Club with so much baggage and camping equipment that it took 11 canoes to take them to their campsite. Then, fearing a cold night, they sent back for extra blankets involving another long journey for a canoe.

The next day, four telegrams arrived for them, at intervals, requiring four canoe journeys to deliver them. The first telegram was from the nurse of little Vinson: "Vinson sneezed this morning so I have sent for the doctor." The second telegram was from the doctor: "I was called to examine your son. I found no fever or any unfavourable symptoms." The third telegram was from the nurse: "Doctor has been and says Vinson is alright." The fourth telegram was from Mr McLean's secretary: "All telegrams and letters must be forwarded to Mr McLean at all costs."

Edward McLean was the owner of the Hope Diamond which he had bought from Pierre Cartier for $180,000 after some prevarication, as the diamond had a reputation for bringing bad luck to the owner. Sure enough the McLean's son, Vinson aged 9, was struck by a car and killed whilst crossing the road outside their Washington home in 1919 and Edward McLean became mentally ill. Evalyn eventually sued her husband for divorce when his behaviour became increasingly erratic; he re-married and moved to Riga, Latvia, and the Washington Post was sold.

Moose Hunt in September 1914

I had a welcome break in September 1914 from a spell of some of the longest days of mental effort I had experienced. My firm had arranged a moose-hunt for an American client, and I was asked to go with him as a 'bear leader' because of my experience of moose-hunting and of bush life.

This trip, my last, was however entirely different from winter stalking in the snow in Manitoba. To reach the Wayagamack timber limits, we travelled by train then motorboat, towing a scow with horse and cart (in pieces) and our stores on board. We stayed the first night in a French-Canadian house beside some rapids on the St Maurice and reached Rat River hamlet on the edge of the Wayagamack property the following afternoon. There, with McKenzie and Allard as our guides, we loaded the horse drawn cart and made our way, with much walking along miles of rough track, to our camp where the tent was already erected on the swampy shores of a pretty lake. Fine lake trout, easily caught with both fly and bait, provided us with tasty meals.

Moving to a larger lake the next day Allard, the French-Canadian guide, used a birch bark horn at dusk to call the bull moose by imitating the love call of a cow moose. Waiting silently and nervously, behind the point of land, with rifles at the ready was exciting, but we were disappointed. Another half-hour of 'calling' at daybreak the next morning produced only the distant reply of a bull moose who was doubtless suspicious and did not turn up. The day was spent in a long trudge through dense forest to a third lake with a timber dam and sluice at its outlet. Progress was terribly slow over fallen trees. In Canadian virgin forest there are generally more fallen trees, in various stages of decay, than standing ones, unlike in an East African forest, where white ants keep the forest floor perfectly clean of the debris of trees making it possible to move more easily.

Calling moose at dusk, on our last day, and again on the morning of our departure produced no results. Allard's moose call was probably a poor imitation of the real love call and deceived no bull moose.

The whole trip was none the less enjoyable or colourful and we made

Allard using birch bark horn to call moose

our way back, beginning with a 5-mile tramp to Rat River, and then to the railway which brought us back to civilisation and Montreal.

Spitting

During this last moose hunt Allard was spitting dark coloured tobacco juice every few minutes, all day long. I looked forward to the night-time when the spitting would stop. But not a bit of it, as he lay alongside me on his back in the tent, he continued to spit, shooting it beyond his feet! This, in a nightmare which I had that night, caused a flood in the tent and the prospect of a ghastly end.

Spitting, as a habit especially in French-Canadian cities, always shocked me and I never got used to the pollution that it caused. Chewing tobacco was the principal cause, also catarrh, which, contracted in winter in over-dry rooms, often lasted throughout the year. Spittoons were, of course, provided in all drinking bars and even in some lounges.

A highway by-law in Montreal threatened a heavy fine for spitting on the sidewalks. This meant waiting till one came to a cross street, which therefore became even more disgusting. On the street-cars were notices reading 'He who expectorates on these cars cannot expect to rate as a gentleman.' Another notice seen in a public building read 'Gentlemen will not, and others must not spit on these premises.'

Appointment as Chief Designer for a new Canadian Kodak Factory in Toronto

In June 1914 I was appointed chief designer for the large reinforced concrete factory buildings for the new Canadian Kodak factory in North Toronto. This was the last and most important of my jobs in Canada. I had a staff of three designers, only one of whom was qualified, and 12 draughtsmen.

The Canadian Kodak factory in Toronto for which I was Chief Designer

Because the main contractor wanted the detailed drawings of the foundations before winter set in, we had to work exceptionally long hours, sometimes starting at 4.30 am, even on Saturdays. I put in many hours of overtime and sometimes spent every other night in the office, resting for only 4 hours after midnight on the carpeted floor of my boss's office. Of course, I received no extra pay, or even thanks for my efforts.

In addition to the factory buildings, the project included a 250 feet diameter water tank for which I designed a special elastic seal between the 10 ft high retaining wall and the floor. The design proved successful and the company reported later that the cost of repairs had been only five dollars in 5 years.

When visiting my old firm Pringles 10 years later in 1924 on my way back home from Mesopotamia, I was introduced to new members of the staff as 'the engineer who went to bed only every other night when there was a rush job to be done'.

I did not see these buildings after they were built until exactly 50 years later, in September 1964, when I travelled across Canada with my son, Brian, who had been working during his College vacation for CIL in Brownsburg, near Lachute in Quebec.

The reinforced concrete buildings under construction in 1914

One of the completed buildings for the Kodak Factory in Toronto

Outbreak of the First World War and Departure for England

War in Europe was declared between Austria-Hungary and Serbia on 28th July 1914 and, when Britain declared war on Germany on 4th August, contingents of Canadians were formed in support of the home country. On 28th September I joined No.5 (Business and Professional Men's) Company of the Westmount Rifles in Montreal, comprising people like myself volunteering for spare time drilling. A few weeks later, after an examination, I was promoted to NCO rank. We had drills and lectures most evenings after work, but we never saw a rifle or a uniform.

127th Battalion, CEF, on Parade at Kodak Heights
before the Great War

Frank de Jong had become my best pal in Montreal, and we would take my canoe out on the river on a Saturday afternoon and have a picnic. He and I were sometimes invited to his uncle Philip Lahee's place in Hudson Heights for a Sunday lunch party. Philip ran an electrical engineering company in which he employed Frank, and the Lahees became my good friends. They were amongst the many Canadians with whom I kept in touch and exchanged Christmas letters every year.

During my absence on the moose-hunt that September, only weeks after war broke out, Frank joined up and sailed to the UK with the First Canadian contingent of 35,000 officers and men, mostly of English or Scottish birth.

By early November my work was thinning down considerably, and I was having difficulty in finding jobs for my assistants. This added to my frustration at the lack of any prospect of an early commission and of sailing to Europe with a Second Canadian contingent. I was already over 31 years old and impatient to join up and make my contribution to the war effort. So I paid Dr Nelson for a medical examination to check that I was fit for active service overseas and I had a meeting with the Adjutant who advised that it might be quicker to try for a commission in England. As soon as I received a clear medical report, I decided to throw up my job with Pringles and to pay my own passage home to join up there.

During my last few weeks in Canada I continued to train with the Westmount Rifles, attending drill parades and going on field exercises in freezing temperatures. We also held a 'Great Patriotic Concert' on 6th November to raise money for the Company. Ironically, just before I left Canada I received a letter offering me a provisional lieutenancy in the Westmount Rifles and the opportunity to apply for overseas service, but it was too late, I had already made my decision and bought my ticket.

I collected my belongings from the Cartierville Canoe Club, but sadly had to leave my canoe there. I handed in my notice to my landlady Miss Pipe, bought Christmas presents for all my friends in Montreal and said goodbye.

On 24th December I left Montreal by train for New York where I spent Christmas Day, putting up for two nights in the McAlpin Hotel, a new 25 storey building on the corner of Broadway and 34th Street. It could accommodate 2,500 guests and was the largest hotel in the world when it was completed in 1912. I visited Madison Square, the new City Hall and the Aquarium before visiting the Woolworth Building; built in 1913 it was a pioneering building which changed the New York skyline. The tallest building in the world until 1930, it was the first great monument of the American perpendicular age and provided a wonderful view over the city from the 58th floor (750 ft high). It was the headquarters and vertical manifestation of an empire built on five-and-dime stores by Frank Winfield Woolworth, appealing to ordinary shoppers with cheap products piled high and paid for in cash. After dinner I completed my day in New York with a visit to the Hippodrome Theatre, also billed as the largest in the world with a seating capacity of 5,300.

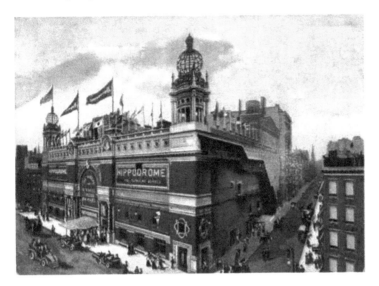

The Hippodrome, New York, in 1914

The next day, Boxing Day, I boarded the American liner, USMS St Louis (11,600 tons), having no difficulty in obtaining a second class berth. The total cost of my journey from Montreal to my parent's home in Wenham was $118 including all meals and expenses, $10 for my two nights and a day in New York and $10 for excess baggage charges, leaving me with just $562 to my name! And so ended my 7 years in Canada.

The McAlpin Hotel, 25 storeys high, was the
largest in the world at the time

Topping out the 60-storey
Woolworth Building which was
the tallest in the world from
1913-1930

Photos of me in Montreal in 1914

Return to Canada in 1924 on my way home from Mesopotamia and my final visit in 1964

After serving in France and Belgium during the First World War from 1914 until 1919, I was assigned to the British Army of Occupation in Mesopotamia for 4 years. When I was demobilised in May 1924 I sailed from Basra to Bombay where I was lucky to catch a Round-the-World cruise ship, The Empress of Canada, just as it was about to leave for Vancouver. It was a most interesting voyage stopping in Rangoon, Singapore, Indonesia, the Philippines, Hawaii and Japan before we arrived in Vancouver on 24th May.

I spent a couple of nights in the Hotel Vancouver, taking a sightseeing tour of Stanley Park and the City and meeting up with my old friends C.B. Pearson and W.W. Willis. Willis drove me to the Capilano Canyon to see the suspension bridge, originally built in 1889 of hemp ropes and cedar decking but replaced in 1903 with a wire cable bridge. Pearson joined me for dinner, and we talked for hours in my room until I walked with him back to the ferry to his home in North Vancouver at midnight.

The next day I took the train to Kamloops to see Aunt Agnes and her husband Charlie Green. Charlie came with Tom Lott to the hotel to pick me up in his Ford car and take me to their home in Rose Hill where I had dinner, more long chats and stayed the night. Charlie showed me round his two ¼ sections the next day to see his cattle and horses; his crops the previous year had been poor having been attacked by grasshoppers. I then went with Aunt Agnes to Notch Hill to meet more cousins, Arthur Barnard, Doris Syms and Katie Dunne.

When Arthur arrived in Canada in 1903 he had originally settled in Calgary, but he found the winters there too harsh and had moved up to the Kamloops district where he had selected a vacant block of Crown land in Blind Bay, on the edge of Shushwap Lake. One could obtain a block of land for agricultural development through a process involving Pre-emption followed by a Certificate of Improvement once the land had been developed. Arthur had chosen his block in Blind Bay for its permanent water and milder climate in order to establish an orchard there, but it was at the northern-most end of the region suitable for fruit growing. He had probably been too late to acquire a block further south in the Okanagan Valley which would have been much more productive.

When his mother died in 1904, his father and his siblings came out to Canada to join him. Arthur's twin sister Katie had married Walter Dunne and they gave us a warm welcome in their fine home in Notch Hill. Arthur then took me to Blind Bay to meet his wife Christina, their 19 month old son Frank, and his father, my Uncle Frank Barnard. They proudly showed me around their farm buildings, their peach, cherry and apple orchards and the latest clearings, sampling his excellent cider before we joined up with Arthur's brother Leslie and his younger sister, Doris Syms and her son Teddie aged 7.

After a night with Arthur in Blind Bay he drove me the next morning in a 'Democrat' with 2 horses back to Notch Hill to catch the CPR train for Banff. Doris and little Teddie accompanied me as far as Salmon Arm where she was living; I went on to Banff where I checked in for two nights in the world-famous Banff Springs Hotel built by the Canadian Pacific Railway company. It had a swimming pool in the forecourt heated by the hot springs and was known for its 'million dollar' view over the Bow River valley.

Photo of Banff Springs in 1924 taken from part-way
up Sulphur Mountain to capture the 'million dollar
view' down the Bow River Valley

THE BANFF SPRINGS HOTEL
AND BOW VALLEY

An especially fine view of the hotel, the golf course, and the Fairholme Range on the
skyline. The river has eroded its valley between Tunnel and Rundle Mountains, which
in early geological time formed a continuous ridge.

Banff Springs Hotel brochure – 1964

The trip across the Rockies was spectacular and has been likened to travelling through fifty Switzerlands rolled into one. I regretted spending only one full day in Banff; the weather was perfect, and I hardly had time to visit all the sights and enjoy the clear mountain atmosphere before catching the next train to Winnipeg. I found the train very hot, as the hotel had been, but it did have an observation platform where I could sit out until dark, only going in for meals.

I arrived in Winnipeg on 1st June and was met by Gerald Mossman and C.A. Clendenning who put me up for my four nights in the city. During my visit I caught up with Glassco, Chace, Scott, Carruthers, and Brereton amongst several others. Marjorie Coombes, now married to P.V. Torrance, gave me a wonderful welcome and lunch before I called on Laurence Taylor and his family. They were more than surprised when I rang them up and invited them to join me for dinner at the Royal Alexandra Hotel, having seen a newspaper report

Indian Charged With Murder

Juneau, Alaska, Aug. 8.—Willie Jackson, an Indian, was arrested here today charged with the murder of Captain Harry C. Lott. It is claimed that Jackson killed Lott because Lott would not give him home brew beer.

that "Captain Harry C Lott" had been murdered by an Indian in Alaska. Their son Conrad who was now 20 years old and my godson Cyril, just 10 years old, also joined us.

The next day I called on Lady Nanton whose husband, Sir Augustus, I had enjoyed talking to on the world cruise. He had died that summer soon after returning home. I mention the sad fact because, at the dinner party given by the Nantons in Manila, he had been the first to get up from the table at which there happened to be thirteen people. Lady Nanton, answering my question at the time, said that he had probably gone to look for the missing guest! Thus his death supported the ridiculous superstition that the first person to rise from a party of 13 dies within the year.

When I left the Clendennings I went by train via Red River and East Selkirk to Lac du Bonnet and then, reliving old memories, I took a speeder to Pointe du Bois where I was shown over the Powerhouse, now fully operational. Then back to Lac du Bonnet and on to a construction camp of the Great Falls Hydro-electric development a little further down the Winnipeg River where I spent my last night in Manitoba.

From there I went to Fort William, Ontario, where I spent the night before boarding a steamer to cross the Great Lakes. 'A very enjoyable 45-hour passage with a break at Sault Sainte Marie for a walk through the town. We disembarked at Port Nicoll for the 3 hour train journey to Toronto.'

Transferring from the Great Lakes Steamer to the
train at Port McNicoll

In Toronto I was entertained by Mrs Chace, who drove me round
the city to see the new buildings before I left for Montreal and
visits to more pre-war friends there.

My hostess, Mrs W.G. Chace, in Toronto

In Montreal Alec Doherty met me at Windsor Station and we had
breakfast before George Shearer came to pick me up and take me

to his home where I stayed for the next 8 nights with his family. During that week in Montreal I caught up with Harold Jenkins, Philip and Mrs Lahee, Bernard Collett and the Rose family, Guy Wynn, Costigan as well as Harry and Mrs Cutmore and Ella who was then 27.

On 18th June I left Montreal for Quebec and boarded the CPR liner S.S. Empress of France bound for Cherbourg and Southampton.

SS Empress of France (formerly SS Alsatian); 18,481 tons, 571 feet in length. The ship was converted from coal to oil after my voyage in 1924

Of the £500 (all in £5 notes) which I had taken from Bombay for personal out-of-pocket expenses, I arrived back in England with £125. This money I invested in The Consolidated Mining and Smelting Company of Canada and sold the shares 15 months later for £537, thus recovering more than I had spent on my trip! In this very lucky gamble I had acted upon a tip given to me by a stranger on the train in British Columbia, but against the advice of my Montreal friends who thought that the future had already been discounted in the price I paid for them.

Final Visit to Canada in 1964

My last visit to Canada was 40 year later in September 1964. Then aged 81, I flew to Canada to join my son Brian, who had just finished two months' vacation work at CIL's factory in Brownsburg. We travelled across the country by CPR from Montreal to Victoria and back meeting Ella Cutmore, Bernard & Norah Collett (Montreal), C.B. (Bill) Pearson (Vancouver), C.G.J. Luck, Gordon Stamford (Victoria), Marjorie Torrance (Winnipeg), Harold Jenkins (Fort William), Mrs Lahee (Hudson Heights) as well as a dozen cousins in British Columbia. It was a wonderful end to the Canadian chapter of my life and a memorable 21st birthday trip for Brian.

In British Columbia during my visit in 1964